T0196362

To
Know
The Lord is
Salvation

To
Know
The Lord is
Salvation

Evangelist Pastor Ellis

authorHOUSE®

AuthorHouse™ LLC
1663 Liberty Drive
Bloomington, IN 47403
www.authorhouse.com
Phone: 1-800-839-8640

© 2013 Evangelist Pastor Ellis. All rights reserved.

No part of this book may be reproduced, stored in a retrieval system, or transmitted by any means without the written permission of the author.

Published by AuthorHouse 10/07/2013

ISBN: 978-1-4918-2510-5 (sc)
ISBN: 978-1-4918-2511-2 (e)

Library of Congress Control Number: 2013918102

Any people depicted in stock imagery provided by Thinkstock are models, and such images are being used for illustrative purposes only. Certain stock imagery © Thinkstock.

This book is printed on acid-free paper.

Because of the dynamic nature of the Internet, any web addresses or links contained in this book may have changed since publication and may no longer be valid. The views expressed in this work are solely those of the author and do not necessarily reflect the views of the publisher, and the publisher hereby disclaims any responsibility for them.

TABLE OF CONTENTS

FOREWORD

The majority of Bishops, Pastors, Preachers, has forgotten about to teach the Lord God and only recognize God the Father. They forget that it is the Lord God who is God, and it is the Lord who is Jesus Christ, and it is Christ who is the Lord, and it is the Lord that died for the sins of man and not God the Father. That is where they all are lose, like it or not. The whole world knows about His Majesty God the Father; and there are a great number of people that know about the Lord and about Jesus and about the Christ. There are people who also know about the Savoir. However, there are also very few people that Know who, or whom the Lord is. The knowledge about the Lord is not enough to be saved. The knowledge about Jesus, the knowledge about Christ is not enough to be saved. The main reason people talk so much about God the Father is because they cannot explain the certain things, or the events that happen in their lives, or in the lives of others they may see or know. So the recognition is then given to the unexplained Being that is call God who is said to be in heaven. Now, the evil one, the great red dragon, that old serpent, called the Devil and Satan, which deceiveth the whole world, does not concern himself with the people that are not using the Word of God at all nor at any time, because he is the god of this world, and the tribute is laid to him when any person use that term god, and not use the term Lord before they use the word god. (II Corinthians.4:4.) "In whom the god of this world hath blinded the minds of them which believe not," so, the person that do know who, or whom the Lord really is, cannot speak any word god except that the word be the Word of the Lord God. Nor can any person that know who, or whom the Lord is, use in any way the word God and therein not use the prefix Lord God, Our God, Your God or My God: A person that know the Lord and who the Lord is will be careful to give praise to the Lord God and not praise to just god alone. The person that know the Lord will Bless the Lord at all time, and not any other that has the claim to be a god. Therefore, if a person give praise to any other than the Lord God; then they have no knowledge of who or whom the Lord really is.

Now just because people talk about the Lord and from time to time they happen to use the name of the Lord, even in the right place, does not conclude that they know who or whom the Lord really is. There are many preachers and Pastors and others that use the word Lord in the sermons and messages they preach or teach. Yet, they have no idea of who or whom the Lord really is. And that is why they can revert back to the use of the word god, because the knowledge of who or whom the Lord is have not been given to them. (II Corinthians.4:3.) "But if our gospel be hid, it is hid to them that are lost:"

DEDICATION

This book is dedicated to all the believers on the Lord Jesus the Christ our Savior. And to every person that hath an ear to hear the unfolding mystery of the hidden Word the knowledge of the Lord God.

This book is written and dedicated to all who would to be informed that the Lord God is jealous about the fact of people giving the recognition of His work and of His doing to someone else that have done and is doing none of the thing that are being done by the Lord God.

This book is dedicated to every person that will believe and receive that the Lord Jesus Christ gave the power and authority on this earth to His Majesty King James to translate the Holy written scriptures from all the languages and tongues, and compile them into one book, pronounce, decree and declare this compilation to be call the Holy Bible, and appoint this Holy Bible to be read in Churches. Therefore this book is formulated from the Word of the Old and New Testament translated out of the original tongues and diligently compared and revised by His Majesty King James's special command; which is APPOINTED TO BE READ IN CHURCHES. The AUTHORIZED KING JAMES VERSION of the Holy Bible.

Therefore, all things is Nothing But The Lord.

(John.6:47.)
"Verily, Verily, I say unto you, he that believeth on Me hath everlasting life."

CHAPTER 1

WHO IS THE LORD

The entirety of the salvation of mankind is totally predicated upon the knowledge of who or whom the Lord really is. The scriptures in the Holy Bible, the Authorized King James Version tells mankind that in (Roman.10:13.) "For whosoever shall call upon the name of the Lord shall be saved." that there is a fact that when you call upon the name of the Lord you will be saved and there is no force or power that can stop or change that fact. Now you cannot call upon the name of God and be saved, you cannot call God and be saved because there is no other name given whereby mankind can be saved other than the name of the Lord Jesus Christ, and He, the Lord Jesus the Christ our savior is God. Therefore, having the knowledge and knowing who or whom the Lord really is, really is the qualification for a person to enter into the existences of another heaven and earth of which is the completion of salvation for mankind. And it is the promise of which was given by the Lord in (II Peter.3:13.) "Nevertheless we, according to His promise, look for new heavens and a new earth, wherein dwelleth

<u>righteousness.</u>" so then to know who or whom the Lord is gives salvation.

First of all we need to know that the Lord is the Word that came out of the mouth of His Majesty God the Father, of whom the first Person in the Triune Godhead, and has the Authority of His Majesty God the Father to do all the will of His Majesty God the Father and the works: His Majesty God the Father is the Person that thought up the entire creation of every thing that was and is created. Now the thoughts of His Majesty God the Father, are living spirit beings that was put into existence just from the thoughts of His majesty God the Father thinking of it. That is how all spirit beings and every living thing physicality and spiritual, were brought into existence: Now, from the mind of His Majesty God the Father, of whom is the first person in the Triune Godhead, came froth the work that was needed to be done in heaven and in earth; and all that work was done only by the Living Word of His Majesty God the Father, of whom is the Second Person in the Triune Godhead, and is the Living Person Being that proceeded out of the mouth of His Majesty God the Father. And the Living Word of His Majesty God the Father is the One Person that after all the thoughts of His Majesty God the Father had been put into existence, did do all the work that put every thing that is spiritually and physically present, in the place that they are suppose to be. (Genesis.2:5.) "And every plant of the field before it was in the earth, and every herb of the field before it grew: for the Lord God had not caused it to rain upon the earth, and there was not a man to till the ground." Now in the book of Genesis the first chapter and the first verse through to the thirty first verse, every where in the scripture that you see that God said; it is the Word of His Majesty God the Father who is the Person that is doing the work of what was said: Every where in the scripture that you see that God created; it is His Majesty God the Father who is the Person that is doing the thinking, and it is the Word of His Majesty God the Father who is the Person that is bringing every thing from the mind of His Majesty God the Father into the spiritual supernatural ream of the Spirit World: Every where in the scripture that you see that God saw; it is the Word of His Majesty God the Father who is making every thing visible to His Majesty God the Father: Every where in the scripture that you see that God divided; it is the Word of His Majesty God the Father who is doing the dividing: Every where in the scripture that you see that God called; it is the Word of His Majesty God the Father who is making the sound that is doing the calling for His Majesty God the Father: Therefore, (John.1:3.) "All

3

<u>things were made by Him; and without Him was not any thing made that was made.</u>" the gospel writer who is call the beloved disciple is declaring to us that it is the Word of His Majesty God the Father that is the Person who did all of the commands that was given by His Majesty God the Father when the creation of all things were created, and is doing that same thing even now. Now, the first sound of speech was made from the Triune Godhead by His Majesty God the Father when His Majesty God the Father call for the light to be put into existence. There was no conversation but the communication of the thoughts and the will of His Majesty God the Father to His only Word and His only Spirit. (<u>Genesis.1:3.</u>) "<u>And God said, let there be light: and there was light</u>." This is the first Word that was spoken by His Majesty God the Father, and out of the mouth of His Majesty God the Father proceeded the Living Spirit Person of whom is the Second Person in the Triune Godhead and of whom is <u>Word of God</u>: It is the Word of God, that put light into existence. It is the Word of God that made the light and divided the light from the darkness. It was the Word of God that called the light day and the darkness He call night. It is the Word of God that did all the things that His Majesty God the Father had thought up into existence and had said.

Now when His Majesty God the Father spoke and said in (Genesis.1:26.) "Let us make man in our image, after our likeness:" it was the Second Person in the Triune Godhead of whom is the Word of God, that made the Spirit of Man and He made man to be just like They are, which is a Living Spirit. Therefore the first part of Man is the Living Spirit. Also it was the Word of God, of whom is the Second Person in the Triune Godhead that shaped that Living Spirit of Man to look like the Living Spirit of the Triune God. Therefore, the shape of the Living Spirit of Man is the outline and design of the body of Man with out the flesh, and that is the Living Image of the Triune God. We do need to know that Man was made first a Living Spirit before he was a Living soul. (Genesis.1:27.) "So God created man in His own image, in the image of God created He him; male and female created He them." Now in verses (26,28.) the Word of His Majesty God the Father was equipping the Living Spirit of man with all the abilities and sincerities and knowledge and senses that is needed by Man in order to have the dominion over the things of all the earth. All of that was done by the Second Person of the Triune Godhead of whom is the Word of His Majesty God the Father the first Person in the Triune Godhead.

His Majesty God the Father looked at everything that He had made from the though of His mind and the work of His Word and He said it's good and very good. And now that was the six day, and the heavens and the earth was finished. Now, on the seventh day, which is in the time spans of about one thousand years later according to the counting of the years by man, (<u>II Peter.3:8</u>.) "<u>that one day is with the Lord as a thousand years, and a thousand years as one day.</u>" that His Majesty God the Father made a great transaction. His majesty God the Father gave to His one and only Word; of whom is the Second Person in the Triune Godhead, the Authority to do all what His Majesty God the Father will to be done in order to save man and to redeem man back to His Majesty God the Father, when man shall fall from the grace of His Majesty. His Majesty God the Father said that If man would disobey the commandment he will surely die. (<u>Genesis.2:16,17</u>.) "<u>And the Lord God commanded man, saying, of every tree of the garden thou mayest freely eat: But of the tree of the knowledge of good and evil, thou shalt not eat of it: for in the day that thou eatest thereof thou shalt surely die.</u>" Therefore, at the time of the creation His Majesty God the Father put into place the remedy that is needed to get Man back into the grace that Man was created to be into. A great pain came upon the view of His Majesty God the Father that pain was so very great that it put a grieving upon the Triune Godhead, because His Majesty God the Father had said that when man disobey the commandment that Man would surely die. Therefore, when Man disobeyed the commandment it put an unconsole feeling in the present of His Majesty God the Father which made a strong unfavorable breath inside of the Spirit and the Soul of Man. (Genesis.6:6,7.) "And it repented the Lord that He had made man on the earth, and it grieved Him at His heart. And the Lord said, I will destroy man whom I have created from the face of the earth; both man, and beast, and the creeping things, and the fowls of the air; for it repenteth Me that I have made them." Therefore, that prompted the great transferring of the Authority of His Majesty God the Father who is the First Person in the Godhead, to the Word of His Majesty God the Farther, of whom is the Second Person in the Triune Godhead and that transferring made the Word of His Majesty God the Father the Lord God over all that His Majesty God the Father had created: (Hebrews.1:2,3.) "Hath in these last days spoken unto us by His Son, whom He hath appointed heir of all things, by whom also He made the worlds: Who being the brightness of His glory, and the express image of His Person, and upholding all things by the Word of His power, when He had by Himself purged our sins, sat down on the right hand of the Majesty on high:" Now, during the completion period of the great transaction of this great transferring of Authority to His One and only Word; His Majesty God the Father bestowed every thing into the hands of the Lord God and went and did rest from all that had been done and to do nothing any more until it is said by His Majesty God the Father, that the day and the hour of the coming of the Lord God has come and time shall be no more. It will be all over! (Genesis.2:1,3.) "Thus the heavens and the earth were finished, and all the host of them. And on the seventh day God ended His work which He had made; and He rested on the seventh day from all His work which He had made." this is the time when His Majesty God the Father is giving to His Lord God, of whom is the Second Person in the Triune Godhead, the Authority to do as He will Him to do to redeem man back to Himself who has fallen from the Grace of His Majesty God the Father. The transferring of that great Authority which is also seen in (Hebrews.1:2,4.) "Hath in these last days spoken unto us by His Son, whom He appointed heir of all things, by whom also He made the world; who being the brightness of His glory, and express image of His person, and upholding all things by the Word of His power, when He had by Himself purged our sins, sat down on the right hand of the Majesty on high; Being made so much better than the angels, as He hath by inheritance obtained a more excellent name than they." that name is Lord God; and is now being given, and the Appointing of a great Authority from His Majesty God the Father which is put in order by the Divine will of His Majesty God the Father. The divine order is to make the full adoption of the people that want to live and reign with Him when they reach the ream of Eternity. The first of the appointing of the Authority and the dialog of the Appointing is now given to us in the book of the letter to the Hebrews, (Hebrews.1:5,10.) "Thou art My Son, this day have I begotten Thee? And again, I will be to Him a Father, and He shall be to Me a Son? And again, when He bringeth in the first begotten into the world, He saith, And let all the angels of God worship Him. But unto the Son He saith, Thy throne, O God, is for ever and ever: a Scepter of righteousness is the Scepter of Thy kingdom. Thou hast loved righteousness, and hated iniquity; therefore, God, even Thy God, hath anointed thee with the oil of gladness above Thy fellows. And Thou, Lord, in the beginning hast laid the foundation of the earth; and the heavens are the works of Thine hands:" and this provides the facts that the full Authority of His Majesty God the Father, and the Scepter of the great Power of

His Majesty God the Father, is given and Appointed to the Word of God, of whom is the Second Person of the Triune Godhead, and that proceeded out of the mouth of His Majesty God the Father and who is made Lord God over all things: Now, the Appointing and the Anointing and the Transferring of the Secpter of the great power has been done, and His Majesty God the Father the First Person in the Triune Godhead now is retreated to a rest from all of the work and things spiritual and physical that He had thought up and created and put into existence of this world: (Genesis.2:1,3.) "Thus the heavens and the earth were finished, and all the host of them. And on the seventh day God ended His work which He had made; and He rested on the seventh day from all His work which he had made. And God blessed the seventh day, and sanctified it: because that in it He had rested from all His work which God created and made." And now the Word of God, of whom is the Second Person in the Triune Godhead, which is the Word that proceeded out of the mouth of His Majesty God the Father, is now been made Lord God; and the work of the full creation and all therein and what it Intel, from time beginning to time end, is now put totally in the hands of the Lord God; to do that which is the will of His Majesty God the Father: (John.5:30,31.) "I can of mine own self do nothing: as I hear, I judge: and

My judgment is just; because I seek not mine own will, but the will of the Father which hath sent Me. If I bear witness of mine self, My witness is not true." Therefore, the scriptures must bring to the light the Second Person in the Triune Godhead, of whom is the Word of His majesty God the Father, who is now made Lord God over all, by His Majesty God the Father; and who is now address hereinafter as; *The Lord God*. (Matthew.11:26,27.) "Even so, Father: for so it seemed good in Thy sight. All things are delivered unto Me of My Father: and no man knoweth the Son, but the Father; neither knoweth any man the Father, save the Son, and He to whomsoever the Son will reveal Him."

Now the work of the Lord God begins, now that He is made the Lord God over all, and now that the Lord God is the Sovereign God, and has the Highest Supreme Authority in the Godhead. Now, in the book of Genesis From the second chapter; and fourth verse and through all the other scriptures in the Authorized King James Version of the Holy Bible; the Lord God is the One that is needed to be sought after and found. Believers are admonished to seek after the Lord God before it is to late to find the Lord God; and that time is before the life leave your body and you die. (Isaiah.55:6.) "Seek ye the

<u>Lord while He may be found, call ye upon Him while he is near:</u>" There are a many of people that seek after His Majesty God the Father for salvation; but His Majesty God the Father does not have salvation. There are people that lean toward the name of Jehovah, but the name Jehovah can not give anybody salvation. Now the name of God the Father nor any other names that is given or any other person you can think of or can think to call on can not give you salvation. His Majesty God the Father said if any one, any person, any people would at any time disobey His Commandment, they would sure die. His Majesty God the Father also said that the pay that a person will receive for sin, which is the disobedience of the commandment that is given to us, is death. And His Majesty God the Father can not change his Word. And for that cause the Authority was given from His Majesty God the Father to the Lord God so that the Lord God can make the adoption of all of the people that will believe on the Lord Jesus Christ be redeemed back to His Majesty God the Father. The only thing His Majesty God the Father can do is to Judge this whole world; every soul from what has been said from His Majesty God the Father by the sacrifice that was made by the Holy Word the Lord God our savior Jesus the Christ. So, His Majesty God the Father can do you no good, because His Majesty God

the Father can not change His Word. and also neither can any other name that people call on to be their god, no matter what it is or what they have said. (<u>Act.4:12.</u>) "<u>Neither is there salvation in any other: for there is none other name under heaven given among men, whereby we must be saved.</u>" So, therefore, we must call on the name of the Lord, in order to be saved. (<u>Romans.10:13.</u>) "<u>For whosoever shall call upon the name of the Lord shall be saved.</u>" Therefore, there is no other way to be saved. because no one can come to His Majesty God the Father except, but by the Lord Jesus the Christ, of whom is the Word of His Majesty God the Father that was made flesh. (<u>John.14:6.</u>) "<u>Jesus said unto him, I am the Way, the Truth, and the Life: no man cometh unto the Father, but by Me.</u>" The Power and the Authority for the salvation of man is not even in the hand of His Majesty God the Father. When the transference of the Scepter was made, the duty of bringing salvation to man was then put all and fully in the hands of the Lord God: It is the Lord God, of whom is the Word of His Majesty God the Father and with the Authority of His Majesty God the Father, that made the heavens and the earth. It is the Lord God of whom is the Word of His Majesty God the Father and with Authority of His Majesty God the Father, that planted the fields in the earth. It is the Lord God of whom is the Word of His Majesty

God the Father and with the Authority of His Majesty God the Father, that caused the rain to come upon the earth. It is the Lord God of whom is the Word of His Majesty God the Father and with the Authority of His Majesty God the Father, that formed man of the dust of the ground. It is the Lord God of whom is the Word of His Majesty God the Father the Second Person in the Triune Godhead and with the Authority of His Majesty God the Father, that breathed into the nostril of man, and man became a Living Soul. (Psalms.24:1.) "The earth is the Lord's and the fullness thereof; the world, and they that dwell therein." (Psalms.100:3.) "Know ye that the Lord He is God: it is He that hath made us, and not we ourselves; we are His people, and the sheep of His Pasture." Therefore, the Lord God is the True and Living God and is the Sovereign God, He is God all by Himself. The Lord God has received from His Majesty God the Father the full and the complete ownership of this world when the Lord God was given the Scepter of the great power of His Majesty God the Father. So then the Lord God is the God of all that was created. We who believe in the Lord God were made to be the People of the Lord God when the Lord God paid the ransom for our sins with the Death, the Burial, and the Resurrection from the dead of our Lord and savior Jesus the Christ. (I Timothy.2:6.) "Who gave Himself a ransom for all, to be testified in due time." However, at this present day and time right now, the Lord God is received up into heaven, and is seated on the right hand of His Majesty God the Father. (Mark.16:19.) "So then after the Lord had spoken unto them, He was received up into heaven, and sat on the right hand of God." Therefore the Lord God is God the Almighty. (Exodus.20:2.) "I am the Lord thy God," The Lord is the only True and Living God. (Exodus.20:3.) "Thou shalt have no other god before Me." Our God is the Lord God and the Lord God is a jealous God, and that is why we must be ever so careful to give the name of the Lord God the praise, because it is the Lord God that has made us and not we our selves. (Isaiah.42:8.) "I am the Lord: that is my name: and My glory will I not give to another, neither My praise to graven images." Therefore, the Lord God is the God that should be calling upon. the term God is not the name to call for salvation. The term God is what the Lord God is and not the name to call for salvation. A person can call on god, or call the name god, or what ever name a person want to call or call upon and it will not bring about salvation. Many people will seem to get very upset about this fact, but it does not make any thing to change. Unless a person call upon the name of the Lord God, there will be no salvation found. Many people say "well, you know what I mean" but the

Lord God who is our savior, the Lord Jesus the Christ say for us to let your words, our communication be Yea, yea and Nay, nay, which mean to say what you mean to say, say what you want people to know and what you want people to think and do not say what you hope people will think, or hope they know what you mean, because when you say things and don't say what you mean, you have done a great evil thing. (Matthew.5:37.) "But let your communication be, Yea, yea; Nay, nay; for whatsoever is more than these cometh of evil." So then, if any person or people want to not go to hell's fire, they must call upon the name of the Lord God and believe on the Lord Jesus Christ and by doing that you shall be saved.

Now you can see that the Lord God is the God that made the heavens and the earth and all that is therein. The Lord God also is the God that made time and put it into existence. That was accomplished when the Lord God started putting the plants of the field and the herbs of the field in the earth and of which was created also and at the same time, the generations of the heavens and the earth. When the generation was created, the knowledge of time was then put upon the earth, and it was from the beginning of the generations of time to the end of the generations of time. All of that was done by the Lord God: (<u>Genesis.2:4</u>.) "<u>These are the generations</u> <u>of the heavens and of the earth when they were created,</u> <u>in the day that the Lord God made the earth and the</u> <u>heavens,</u>" Time was created and put into existence from beginning of all generations, then to the very end of all generations; and the process of time begin when the Lord God spoke the curse to the serpent and said that he would be going upon his belly all the days of his life. This is found in the book of (<u>Genesis.3:14</u>.) "<u>And</u> <u>the Lord God said unto the serpent, Because thou hast</u> <u>done this, thou art cursed above all cattle, and above</u> <u>every beast of the field; upon thy belly shalt thou go, and</u> <u>dust shalt thou eat all the days of thy life:</u>" And this is the cause that the Lord God said that He is the Alpha and the Omega, the Beginning and the End; because the Lord God put time into existence and it is the Lord God that will take time out of existence. Now all of this was done after His Majesty God the Father had bestowed the Authority upon the Word of God and had made the Word of God the Lord God over all and had gone and rested: Then the Lord God who was doing all the work and commanding all the angels in the heavens was made known to all. (<u>Revelations.10:5,6</u>.) "<u>And the angel</u> <u>which I saw stand upon the sea and upon the earth lifted</u> <u>up his hand to heaven, And sware by Him that liveth</u>

17

<u>for ever and ever, who created heaven, and the things that therein are, and the earth, and the things therein are, and the sea, and the things which are therein, that there should be time no longer:</u>" *So then the Lord is the Word of His Majesty God the Father, which came out of the mouth of His Majesty God the Father, of whom is the second Person of the Triune Godhead and which has the Appointed Authority to do the will of His Majesty God the Father.* Therefore, the Lord is the Sovereign God and Savior of the Soul of man. The Lord God is whom we must seek out if we want to receive eternal life. (<u>Isaiah.55:6</u>.) "<u>Seek ye the Lord while He may be found, call ye upon Him while He is near:</u>" Now the reason we must call upon the Lord is because when any one, any person call upon the name of the Lord you shall be saved. (<u>Romans.10:13</u>.) "<u>For whosoever shall call upon the name of the Lord shall be saved.</u>" When you believe this and you are baptized, you shall be saved; but if you believe not you shall be damned.

Many people use the word god trying to imply that the word that they are using is the Word of His Majesty God the Father; of whom is the First Person in the Triune Godhead. (<u>I John.5:7</u>.) "<u>For there are three that bear record in heaven, the Father, the Word, and the Holy</u>

Ghost: and these three are one." but not so, because His majesty God the Father, the First Person in the Triune God head gave all of His Authority and His power to His Living Word, and unless you Know who the Living Word is, you will not receive the promise that was made by the Living Word for life eternal. (Hebrew.1:2,4.) "Hath in these last days spoken unto us by His Son, whom He hath appointed heir of all things, by whom also he made the world; who being the brightness of His glory, and the express image of His person, and upholding all things by the Word of His power, when He had by Himself purged our sins, sat down on the right hand of the Majesty on high;" So then, the Lord is the Word of His Majesty God the Father and is the Second Person in Triune Godhead, who was made flesh and who hung on the cross, bled and died, and was buried, and on the third day roes from the dead, and is now seated at the right hand of His Majesty God the Father pleading our case for eternal life.

CHAPTER 2

What is the Lord made of

Now the first thing that proceeded out of the mouth of His Majesty God the Father of whom is the First Person in the Triune Godhead, is His Living Blood and then proceeded His Living Water. Now the Living Blood and the Living Water that proceeded out of the mouth of His Majesty God the Father together is the Second Person of the Triune Godhead; of whom is the Word of God. Now, After the Living Blood and the Living Water had proceeded out of the mouth of His Majesty God the Father, of whom is the Word of God; and is the Second Person in the Triune Godhead; and then proceeded out of the mouth of His Majesty God the Father is the full Living Spirit of His Majesty God the Father and who is the Third Person in the Triune Godhead: Also, after the Spirit of His Majesty God the Father proceeded out of the mouth of His Majesty God the Father of whom is the Holy Ghost, the Third Person in the Triune Godhead; Then came the full and complete Authority to do all the will and the work of His Majesty God the Father proceeding out of the mouth of His Majesty God the Father, and that

Authority was bestowed upon the Second Person in the Triune Godhead, of whom was made The Lord over all and is named the Lord God:

Now, The Living Blood is the first supernatural Principle Spirit Element Life Sustaining Fluid in the spirit world that washes away all of the spirit elements that which would prevent or hinder the continuing of life in the ream of the spirit world. (Revelation.1:5.) "And from Jesus Christ, who is the faithful witness, and the first begotten of the dead, and the Prince of the kings of the earth. Unto Him that loved us, and washed us from our sins in His own blood," Therefore, the Living Blood is the supernatural Principal Spirit Element Life Sustaining Fluid that put our sins into remission, so that the flesh can return to dust from where it came and the Soul and Spirit can live. (Matthew.26:28.) "For this is My blood of the new testament, which was shed for many for the remission of sins." so without the Living Blood, which is that first supernatural Spirit Element Life Sustaining Fluid that proceeded out of the mouth of His Majesty God the Father, of which is the first supernatural Principle Spirit Element Life Sustaining Fluid in the Second Person of the Triune Godhead; there would not be forgiveness of sins, and there would be no remission of sins. (Hebrew.9:22.) "And almost all things are by law purged with blood; and without shedding of blood is no remission." The Living Blood is one of the first supernatural Spirit Element Life Sustaining Fluid that was put inside the womb of the virgin Mary, who was over shadowed by the Holy Ghost, of whom is the third Person in the Triune Godhead. (Luke.1:35.) "And the angel answered and said unto her, The Holy Ghost shall come upon thee, and the power of the Highest shall overshadow thee: therefore also that holy thing which shall be born of thee shall be called the Son of God." The Third Person in the Triune Godhead of whom is the Holy Ghost is the Person that put the Living Blood which is the supernatural first Spirit Element Life Fluid in the Second Person in the Triune Godhead; inside the womb of the virgin Mary. Now, it was the Holy Spirit Being which is a heavenly Angel by the name of Gabriel that brought the Supernatural first Spirit Element Life Sustaining Fluid in the Second Person of the Triune Godhead to the virgin Mary. (Luke.1:26,27.) "And in the sixth month the angel Gabriel was sent from God unto a city of Galilee named Nazareth, To a virgin espoused to a man whose name was Joseph, of the house of David; and the virgin's name was Mary." So then, the it was the Holy Spirit Being which is an angel that was sent from God with the Living Blood of which is the First Spirit Element of Fluid of the Second Person in the Triune Godhead, and the Holy Ghost of whom is the Third Person in the Triune Godhead, and the Holy Ghost put the Living Blood, which is the supernatural First Spirit Element Lift Sustaining Fluid, inside the womb of the virgin Mary. Now this supernatural thing that is being done with the virgin Mary, in using the terms and the vernaculars of the languages of today, it would be said that the Holy Ghost made Love to the virgin Mary. Therefore, the Holy Ghost who is the Third Person in the Triune Godhead made Love to the virgin Mary and put the Living Blood, which is the supernatural First Spirit Element Life Sustaining Fluid, inside her womb.

Now, The Living Water is the supernatural Spirit Vicissitude for the existence of life, that supernaturally exist in the spirit world: This supernatural Spirit Vicissitude of life existence is that very Spirit which proceeded out of the mouth of His Majesty God the Father. Therefore, The Living Water supernatural Spirit Vicissitude of Life existence which proceeded out of the Mouth of His Majesty God the Father is the Second Living Element of the Second Person of the Triune Godhead: The Living Water supernatural Spirit Vicissitude of Life Existence is the Second Living Element that was put in the womb of Mary the virgin by the Holy Ghost; when the Holy Spirit

Being' the angel from heaven who has the name of Gabriel, had placed the Holy Ghost, who is the Third Person in the Triune Godhead, and is the Person that overshadowed the virgin Mary, and put the Living Water Supernatural Spirit vicissitude of Life which is the Second Living Element of Life in the Second Person in the Triune Godhead, which is the Living Water Spirit Vicissitude of Life Existence, into the presence of the virgin Mary when the angel said to the virgin Mary that she would conceive in her womb a son, and the Holy Ghost made Love to the virgin Mary and she conceived; (Luke.1:31.) "And, behold, thou shalt conceive in thy womb, and bring forth a son, and shalt call his name Jesus." So then, The Living Blood which is the First Principle Spirit Element of Life Fluid in the Second Person of the Triune Godhead, and The Living Water Spirit supernatural Vicissitude of Life existence, that proceeded out of the mouth of His Majesty God the Father is the Second Person in the Triune Godhead, and His name is called The Word of God: (Revelation.19:11,13.) "And I saw heaven opened, and behold a white horse; and he that sat upon him was called Faithful and True, and in righteousness He doth judge and make war. His eyes were as a flame of fire, and on His head were many crowns; and He had a name written, that no man knew, but He Himself. And He was clothed with a vesture dipped in blood: and His name is called The Word of God." So now, we can know that it was the Triune Godhead, in the Person of His Majesty God the Father, the First Person in the Godhead and the Word of God, of whom is the Second Person in the Triune Godhead, and the Holy Ghost, of whom is the Third Person in the Triune Godhead that supernaturally wrought the supernatural wonders to pay the price for the disobediences of Man.

Now, the next thing that proceeded out of the mouth of His Majesty God the Father, is the Living Spirit of His Majesty God the Father, and the Living Spirit of His Majesty God the Father is the Third Person in the Triune Godhead. The Triune Godhead is three Person in One. The Triune Godhead is not three personalities in one person, but three Person in One. There are people that say the Godhead is three personalities but it is not so. Now this is declared to us by the first letter of John the Apostle, and he say of whom the three Person are and the position of each; (I John.5:7.) "For there are three that bear record in heaven, the Father, the Word, and the Holy Ghost: and these three are one." So now you see the Triune Godhead: Now, the First Person in the Godhead is His Majesty God the Father, whom is God. The Second Person in the Triune Godhead is the Living Word of His

25

Majesty God the Father, whom is the Word of God. The Third Person of the Triune Godhead is the Living Spirit of His Majesty God the Father, whom is the Holy Ghost. These three are One: Therefore, They three is the one Godhead. <u>They are Three in One</u>. Now, some people who don't know what they are saying will say it suppose to be said the Father, Son and Holy Ghost; and they are one; but that is not so, that is not true at all. The scripture does not give The Father the Son and the Holy Ghost to be the Godhead of the True and Living God; but the scripture does give that the use of the Father and of the Son and of the Holy Ghost is the power and authority given by the Lord Jesus Christ for the preachers and Pastors, and the man of God to use for the Baptizing of new converts and the new believers into the faith of the Lord Jesus Christ, for that only and nothing else can be done by that power and authority. The use of that power and Authority is just for Baptisms only: (<u>Matthew.28:18,19.</u>) "<u>And Jesus came and spake unto them, saying, All power is given unto me in heaven and earth. Go ye therefore, and teach all nations, baptizing them in the name of the Father, and of the Son, and of the Holy Ghost:</u>" So then, there are three different Persons in the Triune Godhead, The Father, The Word, and The Holy Ghost, and these are the three that are one Godhead: (<u>Colossians.2:8,9.</u>) "<u>Beware lest any</u>

man spoil you through philosophy and vain deceit, after the tradition of men, after the rudiments of the world, and not after Christ. For in Him dwelleth all the fullness of the Godhead bodily."

So Now, the next thing that came out of the mouth of His Majesty God the Father is the Authority of His Majesty. The Authority is the power to do all the will and the work of His Majesty God the Father; of whom is the First Person in the Triune Godhead: His Majesty God the Father bestowed the power and Authority of His Majesty upon the Second Person in the Triune Godhead: That Authority of His Majesty, made the Second Person in the Triune Godhead, the Lord and God over all the things in heaven and in earth. Therefore, when the angel Gabriel stood in the presence of the virgin Mary with the Living Blood and the Living Water of whom is the Second Person in the Triune Godhead; who had the Authority of His Majesty to do all the will of His Majesty God the Father, the Holy Ghost; of whom is the Third Person in the Triune Godhead, overshadowed the virgin Mary and put inside the womb of the virgin Mary the Living Blood and the Living Water of whom is the Second Person in the Triune Godhead and bearer of the Authority of his Majesty God the Father to do all the will of His Majesty God the father, and is of whom has the name, The Word of God. Now, the Holy Ghost, the Third Person in the Triune Godhead put the Word of God inside the womb of the virgin Mary; and that is why the gospel writer John wrote; (John.1:1,4.) "In the beginning was the Word, and the Word was with God, and the Word was God. The same was in the beginning with God. All things were made by Him; and without Him was not any thing made that was made. In Him was life; and the life was the light of men." because it was the Word of His Majesty God the Father whom the Holy Spirit Angel who is named Gabriel, carried down to the presents of the virgin Mary and was overshadowed by the Holy Ghost. This was also the writer John's addition to the scripture, and said; (John.1:14.) "And the Word was made flesh, and dwelt among us, (and we beheld His glory, the glory as of the only begotten of the Father,) full of grace and truth." So then, the Word of His Majesty God the Father which has the Authority of His Majesty God the Father, was put inside the womb of the virgin Mary and the flesh from the virgin Mary covered the Word of His Majesty God the Father which has the Authority of His Majesty God the Father, of whom is the Living Blood and Living Water of His Majesty God the Father: Therein, Mary gave birth to a Son, and that has the Living Blood and the Living Water of His Majesty God the Father of whom is the First Person in the Triune Godhead. Therefore, the virgin Mary gave birth to the Son of His Majesty God the Father the First Person in the Triune Godhead; and that Son is the Son of God who is call by the name Jesus.

Now the Son of God, of whom is the Word of His Majesty God the Father who has the Authority of His Majesty God the Father; is the Second Person of the Triune Godhead: He is the Person who left the throne of the Triune Godhead in heaven and was supernaturally born of a human being person, to show every person that will believe that He is the Son of God, will be able to die the death that only removes the flesh from the Living Spirit that the flesh is wrapped around, and take the Living Spirit and Soul, of which is the Breath of the Lord God that is inside the Living Spirit, and take the Living Spirit and Soul and put the Spirit and Soul to rest to wait for the time to come to be put on the New Earth. So then, the knowledge that is being given is that the Triune Godhead is three Person in One Godhead; and they are the Father, the Word, and the Holy Ghost, and these three are One. These <u>three are the One</u> Triune of the Godhead. But the Lord God is the Second Person in the Triune Godhead that left the Throne in heaven and was made flesh so that the invitation to eternal life can be extended to every person:

Now, every Living thing that proceeded out of the mouth His Majesty God the Father, whom is the First Person of the Triune God head, are Living Spirit Beings or is a Living Being Thing. Every thought from His Majesty God the Father, is a Living Being Thing. The trees, are living things; birds, are living things; flowers, are living things; insects, are living things; animals, are living things; fish, are living things; these are all the living things. Every Word that was spoken by His Majesty God the Father, is a Living Spirit and is a Supernatural Living Word. The very Blood from His Majesty God the Father; is a Living Spirit that gives Life; and that is a life Everlasting. The Water from His Majesty God the Father; is a Spirit of Living Water, and that wash away sins from the Spirit of Man. Therefore, every Word that proceeded out of the mouth of His Majesty God the Father, is a Living Spirit Thing:

Now the first thing that had proceeded out of the mouth of His Majesty God the Father is the Second Person of His Majesty God the Father in the Triune Godhead. The Word of His Majesty God the Father is the Second Person of the Triune Godhead and is the First thing that proceeded out of the mouth of His Majesty God the Father; and that Word of His Majesty God the Father is now the Second Person in the Triune Godhead.

Now the second thing that had proceeded out of the mouth of His Majesty God the Father is the Third Person of His Majesty God the Father in the Triune Godhead. The Living Holy Spirit of His Majesty God the Father is the Holy Ghost whom is the Third thing that proceeded out of the mouth of His Majesty God the Father; and that Holy Ghost of His Majesty God the Father is now the Third Person in the Triune Godhead:

The Word of His Majesty God the Father is a Living Being, and this Living Being is a Person, and this Person is the Blood and the Water which proceeded out of the mouth of His Majesty God the Father. That is why the Gospel writer who is call John the beloved disciple told us about the Word in the first accounting of his writing. (John.1:1,5.) "In the beginning was the Word, and the Word was with God, and the Word was God. The same was in the beginning with God. All things were made by Him; and without Him was not any thing made that was made. In Him was Life; and the life was the light of men. And the light shineth in darkness; and the darkness comprehended it not."

The Blood of His Majesty God the Father and the Water of His Majesty God the Father is a Living Person, and is the Second Person in the Triune Godhead; and it is also that Person of whom is the Living Blood and the Living Water of His Majesty God the Father who is the Person that received from His Majesty God the Father the Authority to do all of the will of His Majesty God the Father to redeem man back to His Majesty God the Father of whom is the first Person in the Triune Godhead. When the time had come that man had fallen from the Living Grace of His Majesty God the Father, the Living Word of His Majesty God the Father was put into the Authority to redeem man. Therefore, the Lord God is made of Living Water from His Majesty God the Father, the Living Blood from His Majesty God the Father, and the Authority from His Majesty God the Father; and was therein wrapped in the flesh from the womb of the virgin Mary who gave birth to the Son of His Majesty God the Father, who is named The Lord Jesus Christ; Emmanuel God:

CHAPTER 3

WHAT IS SALVATION?

This is a question that has baffled the minds of many. There are a great many of preconceived ideas as to what salvation really is. Some say salvation is being with god, some say salvation is something that has to be searched out and found in the Churches; some say salvation is a concern for the wellbeing and safety of mankind. However, the Bible gives to the believer the true knowledge of what the salvation from the Lord God really is; and that is to know that the Salvation of the Lord is the Deliverance from the Power and Penalties of sin of this earth; and that is what is call the Redemption; and put on a new earth that is without any sin at all: Therefore, Salvation is the Redemption of Man back to His Majesty God the Father and put on a new earth: Redemption is the activity of the promise of the life eternal that the Lord God made to all who will believe on Him: That promise the Lord God made to all who will believe is the new heavens and a new earth for all that are the redeemed of the Lord to live there on eternally, with the Lord God our God the God and Savior The Lord Jesus the Christ;

and with also the Father, His Majesty God the Father: In order to receive Salvation, a person who is without the old flesh on the body from this world; must be taken and delivered to the new earth. This means that the Spirit and Soul of a person that lives upon this earth must be taken up by the Holy Spirit angel and put on the new earth, with the new flesh, and having put on a new body which is given to every one from our Lord and Savior and God; of whom is the Person the promise of salvation came through to us. Now, there are three things that must take place to make up salvation. The three things that makes and forms redemption are the Physical, the Moral, and the Spirit and Soul.

The first form and requirement for salvation of man is the physical form: Even though the flesh is the second part of the Trichotomated being call man, yet, the physical form is the first in the requirements for salvation. Now the Physical form of salvation is the physical and the cognizant effort of a person to speak with their mouth the Word of Faith, which is the confession of their Belief in the Lord Jesus Christ, whom is the Son of God; and that the Lord Jesus Christ did Lived on this earth; and that the Lord Jesus Christ Died, on Calvary's cross for the sins of Man; and that the Lord Jesus Christ was Buried in a

Grave for Three days; and that the Lord Jesus Christ Rose from the Dead on the Third day morning with all power: (Romans.10:9,10.) "That if thy shalt confess with the mouth the Lord Jesus, and shalt believe in Thine heart that God hath raised Him from the dead, thou shalt be saved. For with the heart man believeth unto righteousness; and with the mouth confession is made unto salvation." This physical form for salvation was given to man from the Lord Jesus Christ, and that was done so that man would give an outward appearance of an inward expression of the full repentance of sins, so that Man could be redeemed back to His Majesty God the Father: This is the physical requirement for Man to be redeemed: (Mark.16:16.) "He that believeth and is baptized shall be saved: but he that believeth not shall be damned." Now, this was not only a requirement for the salvation of man, but it was a requirement also for the Redeemer, of whom is the Lord Jesus Christ: The Lord Jesus Christ had the need to be baptized so that every body that believe on the Lord Jesus Christ will do what is commanded that the believers do. No one is exempted from the requirement, not even the Redeemed Himself; of whom is our Lord and Savior Jesus The Christ: The Lord Jesus had also to be baptized in order to do the will of His Majesty God the Father. The will of His Majesty God the Father is that every believer must be baptized with the Holy Ghost, and the Holy Ghost could not come unless by the Authority and power that was given to the Word of His Majesty God the Father and is the Second Person in the Triune Godhead who was made flesh. The power is the ability to put the Third Person of the Triune Godhead, of whom is the Holy Ghost; into the Body call Jesus with the Authority and the Blood and Water that was raped in the flesh of the virgin Mary, while in the womb of the virgin Mary; of whom is the Second Person in the Triune God head, and is The Lord God: When the Holy Ghost descended from heaven in the bodily shape form like a dove, when Jesus was in the Jordon baptized by John, and lit upon the Lord Jesus, the Holy Ghost abode upon Him and disappeared into the Body of the Lord Jesus and the Lord Jesus was then made to be The Lord Jesus Christ; because the Holy Ghost was in the body of Jesus with the Word of His Majesty God the Father: Thus the Lord Jesus Christ is on the earth: (Matthew.3:13,17.) "Then cometh Jesus from Galilee to Jordan unto John, to be baptized of him. But John forbad Him, saying, I have need to be baptized of Thee, and cometh Thou to me? And Jesus answering said unto him, Suffer it to be so now: for thus it becometh us to fulfill all righteousness. Then he suffered Him. And Jesus, when He was baptized, went up straightway out of the water:

and, lo, the heavens were opened unto Him, and He saw the Spirit of God descending like a dove, and lighting upon Him: And lo a voice from heaven, saying, This is My beloved Son, in whom I am well pleased." Therefore, the first requirement for the salvation for man is to physically confess with the mouth, that the Lord Jesus the Christ, is the Son of God, and is the Lord and Savior of the Soul of man:

The Second form and requirement for salvation of man is the Moral form. The moral requirement for salvation is the Precepts of the Lord God for the Living Principles of righteous conduct; and the ethical attitudes: Now the Living Principle of the righteous conduct and ethical attitude is the Second Person of the Triune Godhead; whom is the Word of His Majesty God the Father, and is who was made flesh and is the outward appearance: The Lord Jesus the Christ has some outward appearances, and those outward appearances of the Lord Jesus Christ is the Living Principles for man to live by. The Living Principles appearance of the Lord Jesus Christ for man to live by is manifested in threefold.

The first Living Principle appearance of the Lord Jesus the Christ is the Person who is the means and a characteristic manner for the attaining of the goal that is established in the commandments that are given by the Lord Jesus Christ unto Man. That Living Principal is the Person who is call the Way: A person can not serve the Lord Jesus Christ in any manner that is befitting to them. A person can not worship the Lord Jesus Christ in the character that is at most, the best and the comfortablest for them. A person must take off the character and the manner of themselves and put on the characteristics, and put on the like manner of the nature of the Lord Jesus Christ in order to have the means to attain that goal which is salvation.

The second of the Living Principle appearance of the Lord Jesus Christ is that Living Principle of whom is call the Truth. The Lord Jesus Christ has in His appearance unto man the Living Principle of whom is call Truth. The Truth is that Person who is the actual conformity of a verified indisputable fact: It is that fact of which is the character of being true. The Lord Jesus Christ is the Living Principle character of being true who is call Truth. The Lord Jesus commands the character of being true to be given to everyone that Believe that the Lord Jesus Christ is the Son of God, and that He Died on the Calvary Cross, and was Berried for Three Days, and Rose from the dead on that Third day morning. This character is therein given unto the believers in the most Holy worship service of Believers, which is call, The Lord's supper: Now, if any one does not believe that fact, then they are of their father the devil, and do not believe on the Lord Jesus the Christ. (John.8:44.) "Ye are of your father the devil, and the lust of your father you will do. He is a murderer from the beginning, and abode not in the Truth, because there is no Truth in him. When he speaketh a lie, he speaketh of his own: for he is a liar, and the father of it." Therefore, the second Living Principle appearance of the Lord Jesus must abide in the Believer.

Now the Third Living Principle appearance of the Lord Jesus Christ is the Living Principle Immortal Spirit that manifest sustained Breath. The Living Principle Immortal Spirit that manifest sustained Breath is the Spirit Being that was portioned over the earth by the Word of his Majesty God the Father, of whom is the Second Person in the Triune Godhead. The Living Principle Immortal Spirit that manifest sustained Breath had some parts of his Being put into every thing that has life. (Genesis.1:20,21.) "And God said, let the waters bring forth abundantly the moving creatures that hath life, and the fowl that may fly above the earth in the open firmament of heaven. And

God created great whales, and every living creature that moveth, which the waters brought forth abundantly, after their kind, and every winged fowl after his kind: "Therefore, the mystery is to know that the Lord God took some parts of the Living Principle Immortal Spirit that manifest sustained life and put portions of that Spirit upon all creatures so that they could be living things: (John.14.6.) "Jesus saith unto him, I am the Way, the Truth, and the Life: no man cometh unto the Father but by Me." The person that will deny them self, and stop the way they were doing things; stop the character and the manner they have of doing things, and start doing things the way the scripture has given instructions, to those that will believe the scriptural instruction to life everlasting; and change the thoughts that they were thinking about things, and think on the scriptures; and how they are the guide through this life to the next life. The requirement of the moral form gives the believer the mental tools to be stable in the faith that is put in the Lord Jesus Christ. (II Timothy.2:3,10.) "Thou therefore endure hardness, as a good soldier of Jesus Christ. No man that warreth entangleth himself with the affaires of this life; that he may please him who hath chosen him to be a soldier. And if a man also strives for masteries, yet is not crowned, except he strive lawfully. The husbandman that laboureth must be first partaker of the fruits. Consider what I say; and the Lord give thee understanding in all things. Remember that Jesus Christ of the seed of David was raised from the dead according to My Gospel: wherein I suffer trouble, as an evil doer, even unto bonds; but the Word of God is not bound. Therefore I endure all things for the elect's sakes, that they may also obtain the salvation which is in Christ Jesus with eternal glory. It is a faithful saying: for if we be dead with Him, we shall also live with Him: If we suffer, we shall also reign with Him: if we deny Him, He also will deny us:"

Third form and requirement for the salvation of man is the Spirit and Soul. And though the Spirit of man is a single living Being and the first created part of Man that was put into existence; and the Soul of man is the single Breath from the Word of His Majesty God the Father, and is the God who is the Lord God; and the Breath of the Lord God is the third part of Man; yet the Breath of the Lord God and the Spirit of Man are a conjoined Living Breathing Spirit Being that exist inside of the Living body of Man; and that is the which is said that Man is the Living Soul. The Spirit is the first created structure and framed part of the design of Man, and is the container for the Breath of the Lord God which was breathed into the nostrils of Man when man became a Living Soul; and which is the Soul of Man. Therefore, it is to deliver the Living Spirit of Man and that Living Spirit Breath of the Lord God to the new earth is salvation. In order to deliver the Living Breath of the Lord God to the new earth, the Living Spirit must be delivered because the Living Breath of the Lord God is contained with in the Living Spirit of Man. The Living Breath and the Living Spirit of Man is what His Majesty God the Father love and want to retain for His own: So then the delivered Living Breath, the Living Spirit of Man, and another Body of Man onto the new earth is Salvation: This is the completed promise of the Lord God to Man for salvation:

CHAPTER 4

HOW TO KNOW THE LORD

People have developed a number of ways to give the idea of how to gain the faith in the Lord Jesus Christ. Many times the Holy scripture is overlooked and the scriptural methods that are given that will help people to acquire their faith in the Lord Jesus Christ is not used. There are specific ways for a person to acquire the faith in the Lord Jesus Christ our God, and be made a Believer. The deceiver has put so very many different types of words in the face of the people of this world, and saying that these are the words of His Majesty of God the Father: They are so very close to the resemblance to the real Word it is very difficult to know the difference in what is Truth and what is not. The scriptural method given for people to know what is Truth and what is not Truth; is to search the scriptures and examine the main source of the knowledge and the authority of the source. (John.5:39.) "Search the scriptures; for in them ye think ye have eternal life: and they are they which testify of Me." In this day and time there are so very many books that claim to be the Holy Bible scriptures that are given to man in this world from His Majesty God the Father, but they are not. Those books that claim to be the Holy Bible are altered by the work of wise men. (Revelation.22:18,20.) "For I testify unto every man that heareth the words of the prophecy of this book, if any man shall add unto these things, God shall add unto him the plagues that are written in this book: And if and man shall take away from the words of the book of this prophecy, God shall take away his part out of the book of life, and out of the holy city, and from the things that are written in this book." Those books that make that claim has been modified with the reasoning of prudent men. (Matthew.11:25.) "At that time Jesus answered and said, I thank thee, o Father, Lord of heaven and earth, because thou hast hid these things from the wise and prudent, and hast revealed them unto babes." Those books that have the claim on them to be the Holy Bible are fill with the scientific knowledge that can sway the minds of many and provide a scientific proof from the measure of their intellect which will not give the knowledge to know who the Lord is. (Luke.10:22.) "All things are delivered to Me of My Father: and no man knoweth who the Son is but the Father; and who the Father is, but the Son, and he to whom the Son will reveal Him." All of those books that make the claim to be the real Holy Bible will not lead to eternal life. (Luke.10:24.) "<u>For I tell you, that many prophets and kings have desired to see those things which ye see, and have not seen them; and to hear those things which ye hear, and have not heard them.</u>" Those books are not the help that is needed to receive life everlasting; they will not help at all. Those books are the dreams and the lies of many that say they have been sent and anointed by the power of the Lord, and yet they can not speak the Word of God, they speak the words from their logical findings. (Jeremiah.23:21,26.) "<u>I have not seen these prophets, yet they ran: I have not spoken to them, yet they prophesied. But if they had stood in My counsel, and had caused My people to hear My Words, then they should have turned them from their evil way, and from the evil of their doings. Am I a God at hand, saith the Lord, and not a God a far off? Can any hide himself in secret places that I shall not see him? Saith the Lord. Do not I fill heaven and earth? Saith the Lord. I have heard what the prophets said, that prophesy lies in My name, saying, I have dreamed, I have dreamed. How long shall this be in the heart of the prophets that prophesy lies? Yea, they are prophets of the deceit of their own heart;</u>" There is only one book given to man for this world to know the mystery of the Triune Godhead and His Majesty God the Father. A person can not learn who the Lord is and can not know the Lord God or know who the Lord is if the True Word is not made known. (Jeremiah.23:28,32.) "The prophet that hath a dream, let him tell a dream; and he that hath My Word, let him speak my Word faithfully. What is the chaff to the wheat? Saith the Lord. Is not My Word like as a fire? Saith the Lord, and like a hammer that breaketh the rock in pieces? Therefore, behold, I am against the prophets, saith the lord, that steal My Words every one from his neighbor. Behold, I am against the prophets, saith the Lord, that use their tongues, and say, He saith. Behold, I am against them that prophesy false dreams, saith the Lord, and do tell them, and cause my people to err by their lies, and by their lightness; yet I sent them not, nor commanded them: therefore they shall not profit this people at all, saith the Lord." If the true Word of His Majesty God the Father is not known, the hope of salvation is lost. (Romans.8:24,25.) "For we are saved by hope:" There is only one Word of God that is given for the salvation of this world. There is only one Lord one Faith and one Baptism. (Ephesians.4:5.) "one Lord, one faith, one baptism," There is only one name given by which salvation can be able to be received, and that name is the name of the Lord. (Acts.4:12.) "Neither is there salvation in any other: for there is none other name under heaven given among men, whereby we must be saved."

Now, the One Lord made it possible for the world to be able to know the One Lord, and to receive the One Faith, and to be baptized with that One Baptism. This possibility was made when the One Lord gave to only one King; who is named King James; the one and only Authority to translate the Holy sacred scriptures from all the languages the Holy sacred scriptures were written and put them into the English language one time only. Now with the scepter of authority in the hands of the seated king, there was made the decree that all of the translated books of the Holy sacred scriptures be compiled from sixty six books into one book, which is to be call the Holy Bible, and therein be Appointed by the Authority of the seated King, that this book be read in Churches. This Decree, and the Appointing of this book by His most Excellency the seated King is irrevocable. Therefore, the Authority of the Decree, the Authority of the Appointing of this book to be read in Churches, is given to His Royal Excellency His Majesty the King of Great Britain, France, and Ireland; King James; of whom was at that period of time the seated King of the Authority of the England crown; is as follows: In the summer of the year of our Lord sixteen hundred and three;(1603) our Lord and Savior Jesus the Christ, with all Grace, Mercy, and Peace; in whom His Royal Highness King James a fellow Believer and defender of the Faith and placed his trust; gave the full instruction and Authority to His Royal Highness King James to put all of the Holy sacred scriptures into one Holy book, and to Translate all the Holy sacred scriptures from the original tongues into the English languages, and Appoint that this one Holy sacred book of the scriptures be read in Churches; was imputed to the newly seated King His Royal Excellency, His Majesty King James: Now, in the month of January in the year of 1604 the conference that is known historically as the Hampton Court Conference did convened: The conference was the beginning of the work that was imputed by the Holy Spirit of His Majesty God the Father; and given to His Royal Majesty King James, King of Great Britain, France and Ireland. In the year of our Lord in the sixteen hundred and eleven, (1611) the task of His Royal Majesty King James was completed, and the Holy scriptures from the languages of Latin, Greek, Chaldee, Arabic, Ethiopic tongues, Hebrew, Syrian, were all put in compiled from sixty six books into one book. This one book was divided into two parts and called Testaments; the Old Testament and the New Testament. These two Testaments are the one book that is Anointed, Blessed and spoken by His Majesty King James that this book be call the Holy Bible, and that this book Appointed to be read in Church: All of this is the Newly Translated out of the Original tongues, diligently compared and revised by His Majesty King James' most excellent special Royal command: Therefore, the King James Version of the Holy Bible is the only Authorized Holy Bible that is irrevocable Appointed to be read in Churches, and is given to the world by the inspiration of the Holy Ghost. And all scriptures are given by the inspiration of God: (<u>II Timothy.3:16.</u>) "<u>All scriptures is given by inspiration of God, and is profitable for doctrine, for reproof, for correction, for instruction in righteousness:</u>" This Holy Bible is the one Word that is from His Majesty God the Father. So then, one of the specific ways for a person to know the Lord and to know who the Lord God is, must first have need to know what is the Truth, and what is the True scripture of the Truth? The King James Version Holy Bible is the only one book that is the Truth of the Lord Jesus Christ. Therefore, if you want to know about the Lord, you must Start with the Truth of the scripture which is the KJV Holy Bible: No other book that claim to be the Holy Bible is the Authorized Holy Bible that was given unto Man By His Majesty God the Father to give the knowledge of whom the Lord is. King James is the only person who received, through the inspiration of the Lord God, the tack of Appointing the One Authorized Word of His Majesty God the Father to be read in Churches. Therefore, the King James Version Holy Bible is the Word of His Majesty God the Father that is reduced to writing. Now that you have learned that the Holy Bible is the Lord God Almighty reduced to writing; of whom is the mystery of the Triune Godhead; then the belief in this Authorized KJV Holy Bible is one of the specific ways to come to know the Lord our God.

Now, when believe in the Word of this Authorized Holy Bible, this KJV Authorized Holy Bible, you have the Authority of the Truth of the Holy and sacred scriptures, which is the Word of His Majesty God the Father; and therein is present the need for the search of the Truth of the Holy and sacred scriptures to learn how to not be ashamed but how the rightly dividing the Word of Truth is done: (II Timothy.2:15.) "<u>Study to show thyself approved unto God, a workman that needeth not to be ashamed, rightly dividing the Word of Truth.</u>" The Word of Truth is the Lord our God, of whom is the Savior of the Soul of Man. The Word of Truth is the Supernatural Spirit Being of whom we know by the name of Lord God. It was the Lord God that hung on the cross, bled and died; it is the Lord God which is the Supernatural Spirit Being who is call the Word of Truth that was buried in a grave for three days, and was raised from the dead by His Majesty God the Father on the third day. (John.14:6.) "<u>Jesus saith unto him, I am the Way, the Truth, and the Life: no man cometh unto the Father, but by Me.</u>" Now, to learn of the Lord our God, a person must read the Authorized Holy Bible, which is the Authorized KJV Holy Bible. (Revelation.1:3.) "<u>Blessed is he that readeth, and they that hear the words of this prophecy, and keep those things which are written therein: for the time is at hand.</u>" The specific way to know the Lord is the reading of the Living Word which proceeded out of the mouth of His Majesty God the Father. When the Word of His Majesty God the Father is read the understanding of what is being said in the Authorized KJV Holy Bible, which is the Holy sacred scriptures; will be then divinely bestowed unto whom so ever will seek to know who the Lord is. When the Word of His Majesty God the Father is read, the reader will begin to realize the how it is that the people who was at one time the friends to you will come to hate you and because of what you are reading and believing they will be made offended. You will begin to understand you will be heated because of what is going inside of you. When the Holy Spirit of the Lord our God begin to go inside of the reader, the mind of the reader will change and the reader will become a new creature, because the reader is in Christ and Christ is in the reader. (II Corinthians.5:17.) "Therefore, if any man be in Christ, he is a new creature: old things are passed away; behold, all things are become new." When the Word is being read the Holy Spirit of His Majesty God the Father is entering into the Spirit of the reader, and into the heart of the reader, and into the body of the reader. The more that is read of the Word of His Majesty God the Father, the more that is learned, the more that is believed, and the more the reader is made a new creature. (Mark.13:13,14.) "And ye shall be hated of all men for my name's sake: but he that shall endure unto the end, the same shall be saved. But when ye shall see the abomination of desolation, spoken of by Daniel the prophet, standing where it ought not, (let him that readeth understand,) then let them that be in Judea flee to the mountains:" When the reader begin to learn more the reader is made more and more the new creature. The reader will be made a new creature which is a Believer in the Lord and an ambassador of Christ Jesus Our Lord and Savior and Sovereign God of all. (II Corinthians.5:18.) "And all things are of God, who hath reconciled us to Himself by Jesus Christ, and hath given to us the ministry of reconciliation; To wit, that God was in Christ, reconciling the world unto Himself, not imputing their trespasses unto them; and

<u>hath committed unto us the Word of reconciliation. Now</u> <u>then we are ambassadors for Christ, as though God did</u> <u>beseech you by us:"</u>

Another main specific the Lord our God want the Believers to know is that every thing that is written, and that is said, and that is done by the Lord and Savior Jesus the Christ our God; is done with the Authority of His Majesty God the Father. The written Word is the way to be introduced to the Lord. Before any one can know the Lord, the Lord must be introduced to persons that want to know the Lord. The introduction to the Lord is through the written Word: That is acquired by reading the Authorized KJV Holy Bible, because this Holy Bible is the only True Word of Truth from His Majesty God the Father. This Authorized Holy Bible is inspired by the Holy Ghost, of whom is the Third Person in the Triune Godhead; the translated Holy sacred scriptures into the English languages. The specific is that the receiving of this Authorized KJV Holy Bible into the confident reality that this is the Word of His Majesty God the Father, and is reduced to writing. Receiving this Authorized KJV Holy Bible to your full confidence and your full trust is what is call Faith in the Word; the Written Word. Faith in the written Word is a specific that must be in the heart and mind of everyone that want to know that the Lord is the True and Living God. Thus mystery is that the Lord God is the Word of God that Word was made flesh and dwelt among us and the Word died on the cross and was buried in the grave and rose up from the dead with all power in His hands and the Word was reduced to writing and the Word appointed to be read in Church.

CHAPTER 5

WHAT IS MAN?

M an is the physical container for the Spiritual structure that was created and was designed by the thought of His Majesty God the Father for the containment and for the persevering of the place that is prepared for the Breath of the Lord God. That is the Breath that was breathed into the nostrils of man, and man then became a living soul: This Breath is the Living Breath of the Word of God; of whom is the Second Person in the Triune Godhead, and of whom is the Person which proceeded out of the mouth of His Majesty God the Father: Therefore, man is the person that contain the Breath of the Lord God. Man is the only creation on this earth or in the heavens that has the Breath of the Lord God. The Breath of the Lord God is the very thing that made man special in the sight of His Majesty God the Father. And that is why it is found in, (John.3:16.) "For God so loved the world, that He gave His only begotten Son, that whosoever believeth in Him should not perish, but have everlasting life." The reason His Majesty God the Father love so much is because man has the Breath of the Lord God which is the Word of His Majesty God the Father of whom is given the Authority by His Majesty God the Father, so that the Breath which came out of the mouth of His Majesty God the Father, and then out of the mouth of the Word of God which is the Lord God, of whom is the Authority of His Majesty God the Father, who breathed the Breath part of His Majesty God the Father into the nostrils of man; so that the Breath of His Majesty God the Father should be brought back to His Majesty God the Father and then be put on a new earth that only have the knowledge of Goodness and Righteousness. (II Peter.3:13.) "Nevertheless we, according to His Promise, look for new heavens and a new earth, wherein dwelleth righteousness."

Now Therefore, when the question was ask by David King of Israel in the scriptures; (Psalm.8:4,8.) "What is man, that Thou art mindful of him? And the son of man, that Thou visitest him? For Thou hast made him a little lower than the angels, and hast crowned him with glory and honour. Thou madest him to have dominion over the works of Thy hands; Thou hast put all things under his feet: All sheep and oxen, yea, and the beasts of the field; the fowl of the air, and the fish of the sea, and whatsoever passeth through the paths of the seas." the answer is given in the knowledge of the mystery of the Triune Godhead: and that answer is, that man has a part of the Triune Godhead inside him. Man has a Superior and Natural Living Thing that is the part of the Triune Godhead that exist inside his body; and that Thing which is a part of the Triune Godhead is the Breath from His Majesty God the Father which proceeded out of the mouth of His Majesty God the Father inside the mouth of the Word of His Majesty God the Father and then out of the mouth of the Word of His Majesty God the Father, of whom is the Authority of His Majesty God the Father, of whom is the Lord God. The Breath of the Lord God is a Superior Natural Living Being. Therefore, Man has a Supernatural Living Being that is inside his body, which is the Breath from His Majesty God the father, and that Living Being made man to be a Living Soul. And that Supernatural Being made some happenings take place inside the body of man, when the Lord God breathed into the nostrils of man, and that is what made man a Living Soul. When the Lord God, of whom is the Supernatural Second Person in the Triune Godhead; of whom is the Authority that proceeded out of the mouth of His Majesty God the Father, of whom is the First Person in the Triune Godhead; and did supernaturally formed the man of the dust of the ground: This was the action of supernaturally putting flesh on the out side of that Spiritual Structural Design which was supernaturally put into existence by the thought of His Majesty God the Father, who supernatural is the First Person in the Triune Godhead: and therein, Supernaturally Breathed into the nostrils of man, that physical container that is supernaturally formed from the dust of the ground and is the cover for the Spiritual Structured Designed Container that was put supernaturally into existence from the thought of His Majesty God the Father; of which is to contain and preserve the Supernatural Breath of the Lord God that went inside of the body of man, who was supernaturally formed from the dust of the ground, and also into the Supernatural and Spiritual Container that is for the Breath of the Lord God that came out of the mouth of His Majesty God the Father, and that supernaturally made man to become a Living Soul: Therefore, the Breath is the Supernatural Living Spirit Being of which is the supernatural part of the Triune Godhead that is inside of the body of man. Therefore, the answer to that question, "what is man, that Thou art mindful of him; is, that man has a Spiritual Supernatural Living Being part of the Triune Godhead inside him, inside his body, and no other being in heaven or earth or any where else that was created has that element: Only man has that Breath of which is from the Triune Godhead, and have made man to be a Living Soul: (Isaiah.42:5.) "Thus saith God the Lord, He that created the heavens, and stretched them out; He that spread forth the earth, and that which cometh out of it; He that giveth breath unto the people upon it, and spirit to them that walk therein:" So now *What is man*? (A part from the Triune Godhead!) and is made up of three parts.

Also, it is that man has the Image and the Likeness of the Triune Godhead. (Genesis.1:26.) "And God said, let Us make man in Our image, and after Our likeness:" Therefore, man is in the image and the likeness of the Triune Godhead:

His Majesty God the Father; His Prince God the Word, and His Living Spirit God the Holy Ghost are One; (I John.5:7.) "For there are three that bear record in heaven, the Father, the Word, and the Holy Ghost: and these three are One." and they are the One which is the Triune Godhead: The Triune Godhead is the maker of man after their own image and after their own likeness. Therefore, man in the image of God and in the likeness of God is a Trichotomated Being. Man is a Being that is made up of three parts: Man is a Trichotomated Being; he is made up in three different and distinctive elements; and yet, man is only one person; Man is only one Living Being that is in the Likeness and Image of the Triune Godhead. There are three Living Persons in the One Triune Godhead, and there are three different and three distinctive parts in the make up of the one Living Person call man: Therefore, man is a Trichotomated Being; he is made in the image and the likeness of the Triune Godhead.

The first part of the Trichotomy of man is the Living Spirit. The Spirit of Man is the Living Structure Designed Outline of the Spiritual plan for a man in the Supernatural Living Bodily form. There is no physical presence of man at the time that His Majesty God the Father spake His thought into the Living Spirit World of the supernatural existence of Spirits. (*And we must make note that the Spirit is the principle supernatural incorporeal vital essence in the aspect of life opposed to any of and all forms of matter.*) Therefore, it was the principle of spirit that supernaturally pervades the thought and stirred the action of the Triune Godhead to put into the existence of the spirit world the concept of an existing Trichotomated Being which is call Man. (Genesis.1:27.) "So God created man in His Own image, in the image of God created He him; male and female created He them." This is the Living Spirit of a Male Person and the Living Spirit of a

Female Person, but there is not at this time the physical presence of a male person or female person. There is not any physical matter present. The male and the female at this time only exist supernaturally in the ream of the living spirit world. Now the Living Spirit of man is the likeness of the Triune Godhead. (John.4:24.) "God is a Spirit: and they that worship Him must worship Him in spirit and in truth." The likeness of man to the Triune Godhead is the Supernatural existence of the Living Holy Spirit, of whom is name Holy Ghost; and is the Third Person in the Triune Godhead. The Holy Ghost, of whom is the Third Person in the Triune Godhead, Supernaturally is existing in the ream of the spirit world, and He is the Person that makes the Godhead Triune: And that word Triune means Three In One. Now let us not mistake the word trinity with the word Triune. The word trinity means three; but the word Triune means three in one. Therefore, Man is in the likeness of the Triune Godhead by being a Trichotomated Being: The first part of the trichotomic existence of man is the making into existence the Living Spirit of Man from the Triune Godhead. That Living Spirit of Man is the make up from the supernatural Thought of His Majesty God the Father; who is the First Person in the Triune Godhead; and put the concept of man as a being into the existence of the spirit world. and that Though was created and put into the existence of the Living Spirit World by His Majesty God the Father. and is therein, was made the first part of the Trichotomic man, and that also is the first of the existence of the likeness of the Triune Godhead; which is the existence of a Supernatural Structured Living Spirit Being Outline, Designed to contain the Living Breath of the Almighty God, of whom is the Triune Godhead. So then Man is a Trichotomated Living Spirit Being. And that Living Spirit is the first element and first part of Man.

Now, the Second part of the trichotomic Being call man is the making up of the element call flesh. When man was formed of the dust of the ground, the dust of the ground was then supernaturally made by the Lord God to be the flesh that will cover the Living Spirit Being of which is Man. The male Spirit Being that was put into the existence of the spiritual ream of supernatural life is now covered with the dust of the ground, and that dust of the ground is supernaturally made to be that element of flesh on Man. In the existence of man this is the second thing that took place that involved the making up of Man. (<u>Genesis.2:7.</u>) "<u>and the Lord God formed man of the dust of the ground,</u>" So the dust of the ground was the element that was use supernaturally and made into flesh and put on the out side of the male Spirit Being call man, of whom was thought up and put into existence by His Majesty God the Father. The dust of the ground was use supernaturally to be put on the Spirit of man and not the Spirit of the female. (Genesis.2:18.) "And the Lord God said, It is not good that the man should be alone; I will make him an help meet for him." so hen only the Spirit of man was in existence at that time. It was only the Spirit of the man that from the dust of the ground flesh was formed to cover the Spirit. The dust that is of the ground was the supernaturally made flesh which is the second part of the creation of man. Therefore, the flesh is the second part of the Trichotomously made Person call Man. However, the flesh of the woman was made and put on her from the taking out of the rib of the man. (Genesis.2:21,23.) "And the Lord God caused a deep sleep to fall upon Adam, and he slept: and He took one of his ribs, and closed up the flesh instead thereof; and the rib, which the Lord God had taken from man, made He a woman, and brought her unto the man. And Adam said, This is now bone of my bone, and flesh of my flesh: she shall be call woman, because she was taken out of Man." Man was formed from the dust of the ground, the flesh of man was formed and shaped supernaturally to have the appearance of the shape of what we call a human body; a human Being; a human person: Therefore, the flesh of man was shaped to fit the outline of the Spirit Being: Now the flesh that was put supernaturally on the Spirit of Man was shaped to fit the Spirit Designed Outline in order to create the imagery of the Triune Godhead. But the flesh of the female was supernaturally taken from the body of man by the Lord God and put on the bodily Spirit of the female supernaturally when the Lord God put man to sleep and took the rib from man and made woman. The supernatural taking of the rib and the flesh from the body of man made the body of woman, and from that supernatural creation of the woman, made the existence of every person that live or have lived on this earth from that time on until the end of time. The Trichotomated Being that is call Man made it so that the flesh of all of the people that has lived or will ever live, the second part of Man, the creation of the Trichotomated Being which is call Man. (Genesis.3:19,20.) "In the sweat of thy face shalt thou eat bread, till thou return unto the ground; for out of it wast thou taken: for dust thou art, and unto dust shalt thou return." therefore, from the dust of the ground the Lord God made Man and that dust is the flesh that was put on the Spirit of Man and that dust is the second part of the trichotomy of Man. And that dust will change from flesh to dust when the life of the breath in the flesh is gone and death meets the body of man.

(Ecclesiastes.3:20.) "All go unto one place; all are of the dust, and all turn to dust again."

The Third part of the creation of the Trichotomy of man is the Breath of the Lord God inside the body of the Man. Though the Spirit of Man and the Flesh of the Man was in existence from the thought of His Majesty God the Father, who the First Person in the Triune Godhead; and the works of the Word of His Majesty God the Father, whom is the Second Person in the Triune Godhead; yet, the Man was not in the complete Image and Likeness of the Triune Godhead, because there was no Life in the body of Man. Man did not have a Soul until the Lord God had breathed into the nostrils of the Flesh of man and through the flesh of man into the Spirit of the Man, them Man became a Living Soul. When the Lord God Breathed into the nostrils of the flesh of man, the flesh was made a living flesh. The Principal Spirit Element of a natural life sustaining fluid entered into the flesh of Man and the flesh received the fluid that sustains life and was made a human flesh. The Breath of the Lord God continued through the fleshy cover of the Spirit of man until the Breath of the Lord God reached the Spirit Being of man, where the Breath of the Lord God will be kept and preserved, and then man became a Living Soul: When the flesh of Man received the principal Spirit Element of a life sustaining fluid, the flesh begin to have life. The body supernaturally was made to have the blood and the water that is necessary to sustain life. Therefore, from out of the Breath of the Lord God the life sustaining fluids for the body were put inside the flesh and the flesh received the life and was made a human flesh, and man was thereinafter called a Human Being; but man was not called a Living Soul; he was just called a Human Being. So then, the flesh have received the life sustaining fluids and the flesh have life; and the Spirit of man is a Living Spirit, so the Spirit has life; but yet, there is no Soul of Man: The life of the flesh is not the Soul of Man; the life of the body is not the Soul of Man; the Living Spirit of man is not the Soul of Man. The breath of the Lord God on the flesh or on the body or the Living Spirit is not the Soul of Man. Man did not become a Living Soul until after the Breath of the Lord God had reached the inside of the Spirit Being of Man where His Breath will be kept and preserved; then Man became a Living Soul: Therefore, the third part of the Trichotomated Being of Man is the Breath of the Lord God inside the Spirit Being of Man: Therefore, Man is the Living Spiritual and Living physical container for the Living Breath of the Lord God of which proceeded out of the mouth of His Majesty God the Father:

CHAPTER 6

WHAT IS TRIUNE GODHEAD?

This question, what is the Triune Godhead, is so often ask by the people that have been misled to believe that the word trinity is the Triune Godhead. That belief is so very far from being the truth. This is the concept that was put into the mind of the people who have the desire for the knowledge but without studying in the Word. (II Timothy.2:15.) "Study to show thyself approved unto God, a workman that needeth not to be ashamed, rightly dividing the Word of Truth." Therefore, the people with the itching ears rely on the accumulation of the words of people which are call the wise scholars who say they have the knowledge, but are deceived by the very thoughts of their own piousness. (Ecclesiastes.12:11,12.) "The words of the wise are as goads, and as nails fastened by the masters of assemblies, which are given from one shepherd. And further, by these, my son, be admonished: of making many books there is no end; and much study is weariness of the flesh." Therefore, by the study of the Word from the Triune Godhead it is found that the Triune Godhead is defined to be three in one. This is not the trinity.

The trinity is three individual entities and they are not one. It is not the term trinity or unity that will with clarity give the definite meaning of <u>Three in One</u>. Therefore, Triune is the only term that is applicable to define accurately the three in one. The Triune Godhead is God in the Person that is what the one Godhead:

God is the One Supreme position of Authority, of a Supernatural Immortal Spirit Being, which possess unlimited knowledge and all the power and Intelligence of all Beings, and of all which rules all the creation in every universe: God, of whom is of a male attribute is referred to by the name of Father. This attribute is therein attributed by the facts of the creation of the universes; the worlds and they that are the dwellers therein; the earth and the fullness thereof; and all that which is created, is that what has come from this male attribute the same as does the seed of a male person into the womb of a woman that bring forth a child. Therefore, the creator is attributed to being the Father of all creation. Thus that name is referred to God the Father because all creation came from Him: Therefore, the Father is His Majesty the One Most Holy Highness the Almighty God who holds the Supreme position of Authority, and is the supernatural Immortal Spirit Being which possess unlimited knowledge and all the power and Intelligence which rules all the creation of every universe.

The Triune Godhead is the supernatural existing nature of a Living present Being of whom is the One Majesty Most Holy Highness the Almighty God and Father; of whom is the First Person in the Triune Godhead. The Triune Godhead is the Three Persons that make up the full existence of the One His Majesty Most Holy Highness the Almighty God and Father. The Knowledge of the existence of the One His Majesty Most Holy Highness the Almighty God and Father; is dispensed to this world by the knowledge of the presences of the Second Person in the Triune Godhead of whom is the Living Word Person Being of the One His Majesty Most Holy Highness the Almighty God and Father: And also by the Third Person in the Triune Godhead, of whom is the Holy Ghost Living Spirit Person Being of the One His Majesty Most the Holy the Almighty God and Father. It is the knowledge of the presences and the full existence of the Triune Godhead; of which was made possible for this world to receive and yet not to understand; was by the Second Person in the Triune Godhead, of whom is the Living Word Person Being of the One His Majesty Most Holy the Almighty God and Father; the scripture say, (John.1:1,5.) "In the beginning was the Word, and the Word was with God, and the Word was God. The same was in the beginning with God. All things were made by Him; and without Him was not any thing made that was made. In Him was life; and the life was light of men. And the light shineth in darkness; and the darkness comprehended it not." and also the Third Person in the Triune Godhead, of whom is the Holy Ghost, the Living Holy Spirit Person Being of His Majesty the Almighty God and Father. (John.14:26.) "But the comforter, which is the Holy Ghost, whom the Father will sent in My name, he shall teach you all things, and bring all things to your remembrance, whatsoever I have said unto you." Therefore, the Holy Ghost is the Third Person in the Triune Godhead. The Holy Ghost is sent by His Majesty the Almighty God and Father into this world to bring comfort to all who work and live in the faith that the Lord Jesus Christ is the Son of His Majesty the Almighty God the Father; and that the Lord Jesus the Christ did Live on this earth, died on the cross, on Calvery Hill, and was buried in the grave, and was raised up on the third day and received from the Father all power in heaven and in earth delivered into His hands. The Triune Godhead is the central location of the three Persons that are the record keepers of all that takes place before this world began, while this world is in existence, and when this world is no more and another world begin. (I John.5:7.) "For there are three that bear record in heaven, the Father, the Word, and the Holy Ghost: and these three are one." The Godhead is the central location of all of the mystery and knowledge of the creation, and of the total existence of any thing that was created. (Acts.17:24,27.) "God that made the world and all the things therein, seeing that He is Lord of heaven and earth, dwelleth not in temples made with hands; neither is worshiped with men's hands, as though He needed any thing, seeing He gives to all life, and breath, and all things; and hath made of one blood all nations of men for to dwell on all the face of the earth, and hath determined the times before appointed, and the bounds of their habitation;" One of the greatest of the mystery from the Triune Godhead is that man is the offspring of the Triune Godhead. The mystery is that the Godhead is a Triune Being; which mean three in one, and man is a Trichotomated Being, which mean, in three parts. Therefore, man is the offspring of the Triune Godhead. (Acts.17:28,29.) "For in Him we live, and move, and have our being; as certain also of your own poets have said, For we are also His offspring. For as mush then as we are the offspring of God, we ought not to think that the Godhead is like unto gold, or silver, or stone, graven by art and man's device." So then, one of the greatest mysteries to this world is that how man is the offspring of the Triune Godhead in Spirit and in Breath.

The Triune Godhead is the place of the supernatural existence of the One His Majesty Most Holy Highness the Almighty God and Father, of whom is the First Person in the Triune Godhead. The place of the supernatural existence of the Living Word Person Being of His Majesty Most Holy the Almighty God and Father; of whom is the Second Person in the Triune Godhead; and is place of the supernatural existence of the Holy Ghost Living Person Spirit Being of His Majesty Most Holy the Almighty God and Father; of whom is the Third Person in the Triune Godhead. This place exist in the supernatural high places of the heavens. (Romans.1:20.) "For the invisible things of Him from the creation of the world are clearly seen, being understood by the things that are made, even His eternal power and Godhead; so they are without excuse:" There is no excuse for not knowing where the place of the Triune Godhead is. The world does not know the Lord God but the world does know where the most High God reside. The residence of the most High God is in the High heavens, and that is where the Triune Godhead is also. Just because you can not see the place where the Triune Godhead is, does not give evidence that the

Triune Godhead is not there. (<u>Hebrew.1:3.</u>) "<u>Who being</u> <u>the brightness of His glory, and the express image of</u> <u>His Person, and upholding all things by the Word of His</u> <u>power, when He had by Himself purged our sins, sat down</u> <u>on the right hand of the Majesty on high.</u>" Now it is the Second Person of the Triune Godhead, of whom is the Living Word Person Being of His Majesty Most Holy the almighty God and Father, who was made flesh and lived on this earth among us, and when the baptism time had come that the baptism should take place, the Living Word Person Being of His Majesty Most Holy the Almighty God and Father was joined in that body that is call Jesus, of whom the Lord which is the Word of His Majesty Most Holy who has the Scepter of the Authority of His majesty Most Holy the Almighty God and Father; with the Living Holy Ghost Person Spirit Being of His Majesty the Almighty God and Father, of whom is the Third Person in the Triune Godhead; and was then made the Lord Jesus Christ, because the Third Person in the Triune Godhead who joined with the Second Person in the Triune Godhead made the Lord Jesus to have the one Living Christ our savior inside the body that is call the Lord Jesus which is now made the Lord Jesus Christ, because the Holy Ghost had joined in the body with the Word of God. Therefore, the Lord Jesus Christ is the Living Word Being with the

Scepter of the Authority of His Majesty the Almighty God and Father, and wrapped in the flesh from the womb of the virgin Mary, with the Holy Ghost inside the body of Jesus also. Thus we have The Lord Jesus the Christ:

Christ the Resurrected Savior is the Person who is joined together with the Living Word Person Being of His Majesty Most Holy the Almighty God and Father; the Living Authority Spirit of His Majesty Most Holy the Almighty God and Father; and the Living Holy Ghost Person Spirit Being of His One Majesty Most Holy the Almighty God and Father; who has all come together on the outside of the body of the Lord Jesus the Christ at the foot of the cross: The Living Authority Spirit came out of the body of the Lord Jesus the Christ when the Living Word Person Being of His Majesty Most Holy the Almighty God and Father; spoke, while in the body of the Lord Jesus the Christ and said It is finished. That is when the Living Authority Spirit proceeded out of the body of the Lord Jesus Christ. (John.19:30.) "When Jesus therefore had received the vinegar, He said, It is finished:" The Living Authority Spirit of His Majesty Most Holy the Almighty God and Father spoke the parable through the mouth of the Lord Jesus the Christ when the Lord Jesus Christ was talking to the Pharisees and the multitude of people, and told them that the power of the Authority to lay down His life and take His life up again is given to Him from His Majesty Most Holy the Almighty God and Father. (John.10:17,18.) "Therefore doth My Father love Me, because I lay down My life, that I might take it again. No man taketh it from Me, but I lay it down of Myself. I have power to lay it down, and I have power to take it again. This commandment have I received of My Father." So then, the Living Authority Spirit Being; of whom is the Scepter of Authority that is from His Majesty Most Holy the Almighty God and Father; was given to the Living Word Person Being of His Majesty Most Holy the Almighty God and Father; of whom is the Second Person in the Triune Godhead and who is made Lord over all and put inside the womb of the virgin Mary, and wrapped in her flesh and born into this world and call by the name Jesus; and when was baptized was joined in that body with the Holy Ghost which made the Person who is named the Lord Jesus Christ: Now Christ, who is the Living Word Person Being and the Living Authority Spirit Being, and the Holy Ghost Living Person Spirit Being joined together out side of the body of the Lord Jesus Christ, is the Person who got back into the body of the Lord Jesus Christ to take the body of the Lord Jesus Christ to the Father in heaven. (John.20:17.) "Jesus saith unto her, Touch Me not;

for I am not yet ascended to My Father: but go to My brethren, and say unto them, I asend unto My Father, and your Father; and to My God, and your God." Then the Christ laid the body of the Lord Jesus Christ on the alter of the Father for the ransom for the price payed by the Lord Jesus Christ for the will of His Majesty Most Holy the Almighty God and Father for the redemption of man from his sins in this world. (I Timothy.2:5,6.) "For there is one God, and one mediator between God and men, the man Christ Jesus; Who gave Himself a ransom for all, to be testified in due time." Therefore, it is the Triune Godhead that regulates and controls all of the knowledge, and the power, and intelligence, and all beings, and all the rules of this creation in all things.

CHAPTER 7

WHAT'S THE MYSTERY OF THE LORD

The mystery of the Lord is; How God the Father, who is the First Person God, has divided Himself into Three Living Persons, of whom are the Living Word spoken from the mouth of God the Father, and is the Second Person of God the Father; and the Holy Ghost Living Person that proceeded out of the mouth of God the Father, and is the Third Person of God the Father, and They Three Persons are One God.(I John.5:7.) "For there are three that bear record in heaven, the Father, the Word, and the Holy Ghost; and these three are one." And further is the mystery of how the Living Word who is the Second Person God, was made Lord; and therein is made Lord God over all. (John.1:1,3.) "In the beginning was the Word, and the Word was with God, and the Word was God. The same was in the beginning with God. All things were made by Him; and without Him was not any thing made that was made." And then how the Lord God, of whom is the Living Word of God who is made Lord God over all; (Hebrew.1:2,8.) "Hath in these last days spoken to us by His Son, by whom He also made the worlds; Who

<u>being in the brightness of His glory, and the express image of His Person, and upholding all things by the Word of His power, when He had by Himself purged our sins, sat down on the right hand of the Majesty on high; being made so much better than the angels, as He hath by inheritance obtained a more excellent name than they. For unto which of the angels said He at any time, Thou art My Son. This day have I begotten thee? And again, I will be to Him a Father, and He shall be to Me a Son? And again, when He bringeth in the first begotten into the world, He saith, And let all the angels of God worship Him. And of the angels He saith, who maketh His angels spirit, and His ministers a flame of fire. But unto the Son He saith, Thy throne, O God, is for ever and ever: a scepter of righteousness is the scepter of thy kingdom. Thou hast loved righteousness, and hated iniquity; therefore God, even thy God, hath anointed thee with the oil of gladness above thy fellow. And, Thou, Lord, in the beginning hast laid the foundation of the earth; and the heavens are the works of thy hands.</u>" and was made flesh; (<u>John.1:14.</u>) "<u>And the Word was made flesh, and dwelt among us, and we beheld His glory, the glory as of the only begotten of the Father, full of grace and truth.</u>" and through the virgin woman who is named Mary and who received the Living Word of God the Father into her womb by the Holy

Ghost Living Person, of whom is the Third Person of God the Father; she gave birth to a man child who is the Son of God and is call by the name Jesus, of whom is the Lord Jesus; (Luke.1:27,31.) "To a virgin espoused to a man whose name was Joseph, of the house of David; and the virgin's name was Mary. And the angel came in unto her, and said, Hail, thou that art highly favored, the Lord is with thee: blessed art thou among women. And when she saw him, she was troubled at his saying, and cast in her mind what manner of salutation this should be. And the angel said unto her, Fear not Mary: for thou has found favor with God. And, behold, thou shall conceive in thy womb, and bring forth a son, and shalt call His name Jesus. He shall be great, and shall be called the Son of the Highest: and the Lord God shall give unto Him the throne of his father David: And He shall reign over the house of Jacob for ever; and of the kingdom there shall be no end. Then said Mary unto the angel, How shall this be, seeing I know not a man? And the angel answered and said unto her, The Holy Ghost shall come upon thee, and the power of the Highest shall overshadow thee: therefore also that Holy thing which shall be born of thee shall be called the Son of God." and did lived on this earth for thirty years and was then baptized; "and also, at which time the Holy Ghost Living Person of God the

Father came down from heaven in the form of a dove and got into the Body of the Lord Jesus; and made the Lord Jesus to be the Lord Jesus Christ: (Luke.3:21,23.) "it came to pass, that Jesus also being baptized, and praying, the heaven was opened, And the Holy Ghost descended in a bodily shape like a dove upon Him, and a voice came from heaven, which said, Thou art My beloved Son; in thee I am well pleased. And Jesus Himself began to be about thirty years of age," and at the baptism of Jesus, after Jesus had come strait way up out of the water, and after the heaven had open and the voice had come out of heaven, and when the Holy Ghost had descended and abode upon Jesus and did remained there; that was the first and last visible physical sight of the Holy Ghost on earth. (John.1:33.) "Upon whom thou shalt see the Spirit descending, and remaining on Him, the same is He which baptizeth with the Holy Ghost. And I saw, and bare record that this is the Son of God." Then the Lord Jesus Christ three years later died on a Roman cross and was buried in a borrowed tomb for three days. (Matthew.12:40.) "So shall the Son of man be three days and three nights in the earth." Then Christ was raised from the dead by God the Father on the third day; (Acts.10:40.) "Him God raised up the third day, and showed Him openly;" and is made Christ the redeemer and name Christ the Lord: Then Christ the Lord was then made into the written Living Word of His Most Holy God and Father, and the Authorized presence of His Most Holy the Almighty God and Father and was given to His Majesty King James, King of Great Britain, France, Ireland, and is the great defender of the Faith of Jesus Christ our Lord; to Appointed this Book, this written Living Word of His Majesty Most Holy the Almighty God and Father, to be read in the church. And every person that readeth this written Living Word of His Majesty God and Father will be blessed of His Majesty Most Holy the Almighty God and the Father of all the creation: (Revelation.1:3.) "Blessed is he that readeth, and they that hear the Words of this prophecy, and keep those things that are written therein for the time is at hand." And this written Living Word of His Majesty Most Holy the Almighty God and Father is given unto men so that man may be redeemed back to His Most Holy the Almighty God and Father: (Revelation.22:18,20.) "For I testify unto every man that heareth the Words of the prophecy of this book, if any man shall add unto these things, God shall add unto him the plagues that are written in this Book: And if any shall take away from the Words of the book of this prophecy, God shall take away his part out of the book of life, and out of the Holy city, and from the things which are written in this book. He which testifieth these things saith, surely I come quickly. A-men. Even so come, Lord Jesus." Therefore, this is the facts of the mystery of the Lord, and the mystery is how it is that if anyone believe this Book, this written Book Living Word of His Majesty the Almighty God and Father, which is the Authorized King James Version Holy Bible, and no other; they shall be saved and they shall have receive the knowledge of the mystery of the Lord. There may be a number of people, a number of authorities, a number of preachers and teachers that will say that those other Bibles are just as good and just as real as the Authorized King James Version Holy Bible; they will try to convince you that the book they are speaking of is just as vital a tool of faith in the Lord as any other. But that is not so. There are many book that are said to be Holy Bibles but are not. Those Bibles are books of scriptures that have been rearranged for your pleasure, and for a many number of things; that can stir up emotion, but they can not save and they are not the tools to help any one to be save. *God didn't die, the Lord did*: However, they fail to remember the sacred Holy scriptures that tell us that there is only One Father who is over all. (MALACHI.2:10.) "Have we not all One Father? Hath not One God created us? Why do we deal treacherously every man against his brother, by profaning the covenant of our Father?" They fail to remember the sacred scriptures that tell us that there is only One Lord that can save, we can have only One Faith in the One that can save, and that One Faith can only be put in the One Lord our One God; the one and only savior of the soul of man, The Lord God. (Ephesians.4:3,6.) "Endeavoring to keep the unity of the Spirit in the bond of Peace. There in One Body, and One Spirit, even as ye are called in One Hope of your calling; One Lord, One Faith, One Baptism, One God and Father of all, who is above all, and through all, and in you all." Therefore, by this Book, the Authorized King James Version Holy Bible, you have the book which is the Holy mystery of the Lord: The mystery is in knowing that the Lord, He is the Sovereign God and is our only God: (Mark.4:11,2.) "And He said unto them, Unto you it is given to know the mystery of the kingdom of God: but unto them that are without, all these things are done in parables. That seeing they may see, and not perceive; and hearing, and not understand; lest at any time they should be converted, and their sins should be forgiven them." So therein the mystery of the Lord is the process set forth by His Majesty Most Holy the Almighty God and Father, to redeem man unto Himself: Man of whom is loved by His Majesty Most Holy the Almighty God and Father, is the cause for the mystery set forth by His Majesty

Most Holy the Almighty God and Father. The mystery of the jealousy of the Lord is that many people are constantly talk about what God has done and seem like no body talk about what the Lord has done. The Many people that give God the honor need to know that God the Father did not die for any body but the Lord did. People need to know that all things are done by the Lord of whom is our God and not any other: That is the reason the Lord said for us to not have another. The Lord Jesus said to us if you believe in God believe in Him. That is the way the Lord said to us to give the Father thanks and all the honor and all the praise to Him, the Lord who is our God: So then, to know the mystery of the Lord is to know that the Lord He is the Sovereign God the Savior of the soul of man:

So then, to believe the mystery is to know the Lord, and that is salvation:

Another mystery of the Lord is the Living Spirit Being who is the Authority of His Majesty the Almighty God and Father. The Authority of His Most Holy Majesty the Almighty God and Father is the Living Spirit Being Vested Power of His Majesty the Almighty God and Father for Determinations and Control of all things created in the heaven and earth:

The Living Spirit Being of who is the Authority of His Majesty the Almighty God and Father, is the Scepter of the Righteousness of the Kingdom of the Lord God, and was given unto the Living Word Person Spirit of His Majesty the Almighty God and Father, of whom is the Second Person in the Triune Godhead; and who is made the Lord God: The Living Spirit Being who is the Authority of His Majesty the Almighty God and Father, is the Living Spirit which proceeded out of the Mouth of His Majesty the Almighty God and Father, and is given to the Living Word Person Spirit of His Majesty the Almighty God and Father; of whom is the Second Person in the Triune Godhead: The Living Spirit Being of whom is the Authority of His Majesty the Almighty God and Father; is the Living Spirit Being which is the Vested Power of all determinations and control of all things created in the heavens and earth: He is called the Scepter of the Righteousness of the Kingdom of the Living Word Person Spirit who is the Second Person in the Triune Godhead; the Lord God: It is the Living Spirit Being who is the Authority of His Majesty the Almighty God and Father, that made the Living Word Person Spirit of whom is the Second Person in the Triune Godhead; the Lord and God over all. (<u>Hebrew.1:8.</u>) "<u>But unto the Son He saith, Thy throne, O God, is for ever and ever: a Scepter of righteousness is the Scepter of Thy kingdom. Thou hast</u>

loved righteousness, and hated iniquity; therefore God, even Thy God, hath anointed Thee with the oil of gladness above Thy fellows. And, Thou, Lord, in the beginning hast laid the foundation of the earth; and the heavens are the works of Thine hands." Thus, this transferring of Authority was done while the Living Word Person Spirit was still a Spirit only, and was not yet made flesh: The Living Word Person Spirit could not be made flesh until the Authority to be made flesh is given. There is nothing that can be done with the authority to do so. When the Living Word Person was made flesh, it was because the Authority to make the determination that the Living Word will be made flesh had been given to the Living Word Person Spirit and the Living Word Person Spirit could be put in the womb of the virgin Mary by the Holy Ghost, who was brought to the earth by the angel Gabriel. All things were done and is being done to day by the Authority of His Majesty the Almighty God and Father. The ability of the universe to move about and exist come from the Authority which is in the of the Living Word Person who is the Second Person in the Triune Godhead; the Lord God: The Authority of the Lord God laid the foundation of the earth. It is the Authority of the Lord God that did the work in the heavens. The Living Word Person is given the Living Authority which is the Scepter of Righteousness; from His Majesty the Almighty

God and Father, and the Living Word Person was made Lord God. When the Gospel writer John started his writing, he could see the Scepter that is in the hand of the Living Word Person Spirit, he saw also that the Living Word person Spirit was with His Majesty the Almighty God and Father, and also that the Living Word Person Spirit was also the Authority of the Almighty God and Father. John, the beloved disciple also saw that the Living Word Person Spirit and Authority of the Almighty God and Father was made flesh. The Living Word Person Spirit and Authority of His Majesty the Almighty God and Father was put in the womb of the virgin name Mary, and the Authority for the flesh of the virgin Mary to cover the Living Word Person Spirit was in the hand of the Living Word Person Spirit; and gave power to the body of the virgin Mary to give birth and to cover the Living Word Person Spirit in her flesh. That Living Word Person Spirit in the flesh is call by the name Jesus. (John.1:1,3.) "In the beginning was the Word, and the Word was with God, and the Word was God. The same was in the beginning with God. All things were made by Him; and without Him was not any thing made that was made." also in the writing the visible action of birth was made known. (John.1:14.) "And the Word was made flesh, and dwelt among us, and we beheld His glory, the glory as of the only begotten of the Father, full of grace and truth." After the birth, the Word that came out of the mouth of Jesus was given with the Authority of His Majesty the Almighty God and Father. The first knowledge the people had received about the Authority of the Lord was when Jesus was followed by a great multitude of people from Galilee, Decapolis, from Jerusalem, Judaea, and from Jordan. When Jesus saw the people He went up into a mountain, and His disciples were with Him; and Jesus sat down open His mouth and taught them. When Jesus had finished the teaching the people were astonished at the doctrine He had taught them because He taught them with Authority. (Matthew.7:28,29.) "And it came to pass, when Jesus had ended these sayings, the people were astonished at His doctrine: For He taught them as One having authority, and not as the scribes." The mystery of this saying is that the Living Authority Spirit Being Vested Power of His Majesty the Almighty God and Father to Determine and Control begin to speak when Jesus opened His mouth, on the mountain and taught them. There were no Living Authority Spirit Being Vested Power on the face of the earth until the birth of Jesus. When Jesus was in the temple teaching, the elders and the chief priests came to Jesus and ask Him of the Authority that He spoke with. (Matthew.21:23.) "And when He was come into the temple, the chief priests and

<u>the elders of the people came unto Him as He was teaching, and said, By what authority doest Thou these things? And who gave Thee this authority?</u>" The reason they ask that is because, at that time there was not the Living Authority Spirit Being Vested Power of His Majesty the Almighty God and Father present on this earth until the birth of the Lord and Savior Jesus the Christ. (John.5:26,27.) "<u>For as the Father hath life in Himself; so hath He given to the Son to have life in Himself; And hath given Him authority to execute judgment also, because He is the Son of man.</u>" Therefore, the Living Authority Spirit Being Vested Power of His Majesty the Almighty God and Father was given to the Living Word Spirit Person, of whom is the Second Person in the Triune Godhead; and is the One Living Person Spirit Being that was made flesh by the Living Authority Spirit Being of His Majesty the almighty God and Father, and dwelt among us with the name call Jesus, and is call the Lord Jesus by the Living Authority Spirit Being of His Majesty the Almighty God and Father: The Lord Jesus was then baptized and joined by the Holy Ghost in the body of the Lord Jesus by the Living Authority Spirit Being of His Majesty the Almighty God and Father, and was then called the Lord Jesus Christ. The Lord Jesus Christ hung on the cross and by the Living Authority Spirit Being of His Majesty the Almighty God and Father, gave

89

up the Holy Ghost that was in the body with the Living Word Person Spirit, who is the Second Person in the Triune Godhead; and is the Blood and Water of His Majesty the Almighty God and Father; and the body of the Lord Jesus Christ Died: After the Lord Jesus the Christ gave up the Holy Ghost, of whom is the Living Holy Spirit Person of His Majesty the Almighty God and Father, of whom is the Third Person in the Triune Godhead, who was in the body of the Lord Jesus Christ, by the Living Authority Spirit Being of His Majesty the Almighty God and Father; the body died. Then a soldiers with a spear pierced the side of the body of the Lord Jesus Christ and out came Blood and Water: of which is the Living Word Person Spirit Being who is the Second Person in the Triune Godhead; by the Living Authority Spirit Being of His Majesty the Almighty God and Father. Therefore, there was not any thing done with out the Living Authority Spirit being of His Majesty the Almighty God and Father, that is because His Majesty the Almighty God and Father gave the Living Authority of all things into the hands of the Living Word Person Spirit of which proceeded out of the mouth of His Majesty the Almighty God and Father:

The last mystery we will share with you in this book is the Mystery of Christ the Lord. Christ the Lord is the

Resurrected Savior. Christ is all of the life that was in the body of the Lord Jesus Christ. The Lord Jesus Christ said if the Living Blood and if the Living Body of the Living Lord Jesus Christ is not eaten and has not been drank, then there is no life in you. If the Living Body of the Living Son of God have not been eaten and the Living Blood of the Living Son of God have not been drank, then, there will be no life given in this world. (John.6:51,58.) "I am the living bread which came down from heaven: if any man eat of this bread, he shall live for ever: and the bread that I will give is my flesh, which I will give for the li9fe of the world. The Jews therefore strove among themselves, saying, How can this man give us his flesh to eat? Then Jesus said unto them, Verily, verily, I say unto you, Except ye eat the flesh of the Son of man, and drink His blood, ye have no life in you. Whoso eateth My flesh, and drinketh My blood, hath eternal life; and I will raise him up at the last day. For my is meat indeed, and my blood is drink indeed. He that eateth My flesh, and drinketh my blood, dwelleth in Me, and I in him. As the living Father hath sent Me, and I live by the Father; so he that eateth me, even he shall live by me. This is that bread which came down from heaven: not as your Father did eat man'-na, and are dead: he that eateth of this bread shall live for ever." Now to unfold the mystery to you it this: The Blood and the Water of His Majesty the Almighty God and Father is the Second Person in the Triune Godhead of whom is the Living Word Person that was put in the womb of the virgin Mary. The Living Word Person who is the Living Blood and the Living Water of His Majesty the Almighty God and Father was covered with the flesh from the womb of the virgin Mary by the Living Authority Spirit Being of His Majesty the Almighty God and Father; The virgin Mary gave birth to a Son of whom is the Son of His Majesty the Almighty God and Father. Therein the Son of His Majesty the Almighty God and Father is therein call by the name of Jesus. The Living Authority Spirit Being with the Living Blood and the Living Water of His Majesty the Almighty God and Father inside the flesh that came from the womb of the virgin Mary is therein call the Lord Jesus. It is The Living Authority of His Majesty the Almighty God and Father who made the Living Word Person the Lord over all: Therefore, the Living Son of His Majesty the Almighty God and Father is thereinafter called the Lord Jesus. When the Living Authority Spirit Being, with the Living Blood and the Living Water came together in the Living Body that is call the Lord Jesus; with the Living Holy Ghost; of whom is the Third Person in the Triune Godhead with them; the Living Body that is call by the name Lord Jesus is thereinafter call the Lord Jesus Christ. Therefore, the name for the Son of His Majesty the Almighty God and Father is call the Lord Jesus Christ. The name Christ is applicable when the Three Living Spirits Beings of His Majesty the Almighty God and Father came together in Agreement in one body. (I John.5:8.) "And there are three that bear witness in earth, the Spirit, and the Water, and the blood: and these three agree in One." The Living Blood and the Living Water is the Living Word, and the Living Spirit is the Holy Ghost and the Agree is the Living Authority Spirit Being for the three Living Spirit Beings to be in One Body. The three Living Spirit Beings and the Living Authority Spirit Being to be in One body is call by the name of the Lord Jesus the Christ. The Living Blood and the Living Water is the Second Person in the Triune Godhead; of whom is the Living Word. The Living Spirit is the Living Holy Ghost; of whom is the Third Person in the Triune Godhead. The Agree, is the Living Authority Spirit Being that gives the Living Blood, the Living Water, and the Living Spirit of His Majesty the Almighty God and Father the Almighty Power to be the witness, which is the testified spoken sound upon the earth, that the Body these Living Spirit Beings are in is call the Son of God; and is call by the name of the Lord Jesus the Christ. That is the cause of it is given to us, (Romans.10:13.) "For whosoever shall call upon the name of the Lord shall be saved." The body which is call the Lord Jesus Christ hung on the cross and was crucified. The Living Spirit, of whom is the Holy Ghost, came out of the Body of the Lord Jesus Christ first; and that is when the Body of the Lord Jesus Christ died. (John.19:30.) "When Jesus therefore had received the vinegar, He said, It is finished: and he bowed His head, and gave up the Ghost." Then the Living Blood and the Living Water, of whom is the Living Word was let out of the Body of the Lord Jesus Christ by a soldier that saw that the Living Spirit was gone out of the Body of the Lord Jesus Christ and it was dead already, and took his spear and stuck it in the side of the Body of the Lord Jesus Christ and the Living Blood and the Living Water came out of the Body of the Lord Jesus Christ. (John.19:33,34.) "But when they came to Jesus, and saw that He was dead already, they broke not His legs: But one of the soldier with a spear pierced His side, and forthwith came there out blood and water." Now the Living Spirit Holy Ghost Third Person of the Triune Godhead; and the Living Blood and the Living Water Second Person of the Triune Godhead; and the Living Authority Spirit Being of His Majesty the Almighty God and Father is now out of the Body of the Lord Jesus Christ. Now it is the Almighty Power which is the Living Authority Spirit Being of His Majesty the Almighty God and Father that brought to the Living Spirit Holy

Ghost Third Person in the Triune Godhead; the Living Blood and Living Water Second Person of the Triune Godhead the Spiritual Body which is the Body for the two Living Persons of the Triune Godhead; who is the Living Spirit Third Person Holy Ghost, and the Living Word Second Person; and also the Living Authority Spirit Being to be together in. The Spiritual Body is call the Resurrected Christ. The Living Holy Ghost and the Living Blood and Water of His Majesty the Almighty God and Father together in a Spiritual Body is Christ the Lord: (<u>I Cor.15:42,44.</u>) "<u>So also is the resurrection of the dead. It is sown in corruption; it is raised incorruption: It is sown in dishonor; it is raised in glory: it is sown in weakness; it is raised in power: It was sown a natural body; it is raised a spiritual body. There is a natural body, and there is a spiritual body.</u>" So then, the mystery of Christ the Lord is that the Living Word Person, the Living Blood and the Living Water with the Living Authority together in the Spiritual Body is Christ the Lord, who rose up out of the body of the Lord Jesus Christ after His death on the cross. After the Lord Jesus Christ had died and yielded up the Living Holy Ghost and the Living Blood and the Living Water that was in the physical body, the Living Holy Ghost, the Living Blood and the Living Water together with the Living Authority Spirit Being went into the Spiritual Body that was prepared for them, of whom is the raised Christ the Lord; and went to the worship place, the temple and removed every thing that separated the people from the presence of the True and Living God. The Living Holy Ghost, the Living Blood and the Living Water together with the Living Authority Spirit Being in the Spiritual Body, of whom is the raised Christ the Lord; tore the veil in the worship place, the temple from the top of the worship place, the temple to the bottom of the worship place, the temple into two peaces. It was the Living Holy Ghost, the Living Blood and the Living Water together with the Living Authority Spirit Being, of whom is the raised Christ the Lord; that also went to the graves where the bodies of the Believers in the coming of the Lord God, the messiah, were laid down in death and was sleeping, and He, the raised Christ the Lord, who opened the graves, raised up those Believers, those saints who had died and slept, and let them be seen by many and appear to many people that were living in the city Jerusalem; the place that is call the holy city. (Matthew.27:50,53.) "Jesus, when He had cried again with a loud voice, yielded up the Ghost. And, behold, the veil of the temple was rent in twain from the top to the bottom; and the earth did quake, and rocks rent; And the graves were opened; and many bodies of the saints which slept arose, And came out of the graves after His resurrection, and went into the holy city, and appeared unto many." When the rocks were rent and the graves were open and the bodies of the saints which slept was gotten up; it was after the resurrected Christ the Lord had gone down and preached to the souls that were in the prison of death and kept in the grave. (I Peter.3:18,19.) "For Christ also has once suffered for sins, the just for the unjust, that He might bring us to God, being put to death in the flesh, but quicken by the Spirit: By which He also went and preached unto the spirits in prison:" Now the Body of the Lord Jesus Christ was still hanging on that cross at that time. The Body of the Lord Jesus Christ had not been taken down off of the cross, and it was not yet evening time, and the rich man name Joseph who was also a disciple of the Lord Jesus Christ had not begged Pilate for the body, and the permission had not been given to take the Body of the Lord Jesus Christ down from the cross. However, when the Body of the Lord Jesus Christ was taken down and put in the sepulcher, the Body stayed there under the careful watch of the soldiers that were under the command of Pilate. So the sepulcher was sealed with a stone, and an armed guard was posted to watch and keep secure the sepulcher that no one could take the Body of the Lord Jesus Christ for at the lease of time three days. (Matthew.27:62,66.) "Now the next day, that followed the day of the preparation, the chief priests and Pharisees came together unto Pilate, Saying, Sir, we remember that That deceiver said, while He was yet alive, After three days I will rise again. Command therefore that the sepulcher be made sure until the third day, lest His disciples come by night, and steal Him away, and say unto the people, He is risen from the dead: so the last error shall be worse than the first. Pilate said unto them, ye have a watch: go your way, make it as sure as you can. So they went, and made the sepulcher sure, sealing the stone, and setting a watch." Now it was the morning of the third day when the Risen Christ the Lord had just returned from taking the keys of death and hell, (Revelation.1:17,18.) "And when I saw Hem. I fell at His feet as dead. And He laid His right hand upon me, saying unto me, Fear not; I am the first and the last: I am He that liveth, and was dead; and, behold, I am alive for evermore, A'-men; and have the keys of hell and of death." and was in His Glorified Spiritual Body, when The Risen Christ the Lord went and picked up the sacrifice, of which is the Dead Body of the Lord Jesus Christ from the sepulcher; while on His way to the Father, He appeared to Mary Magdalene; and told her that she could not tough Him because He was on His way to the Father and had not yet gotten to the Father. Therefore, Christ the Lord is the Resurrected Savior.

The Mystery of the Lord is knowing that the Lord is the name of the Scepter who is the Living Authority Spirit Being which proceeded out the mouth of His Majesty the Almighty God and Father, which was given to the Living Word Person who is the Second Person in the Triune Godhead, which also proceeded out of the mouth of His Majesty the Almighty God and Father; who was made flesh through the virgin Mary, and was joined in the flesh by the Living Holy Ghost Person, who is the Third Person in the Triune Godhead; and died on the cross, was put in the grave for three days and was raised up out of the grave, and out of death, on the third day and is given all the power of heaven and earth. Now if you can believe that you can be saved: (<u>NOW IF YOU BELIEVE THAT, YOU ARE SAVED</u>!)

This book is written to give a better knowledge of the Mystery of the Lord:

Therefore,
To Know The Lord Is Salvation

If you can believe this mystery of the Lord our God, you will be saved; if you do not believe this mystery you shall be damned: (Mark.16:16.) "He that Believeth and is baptized shall be saved; but he that believeth not shall be damned." This is the mystery that must be accepted and believed by faith, and with no doubting that this is the food for the soul. (Romans.14:23.) "And he that doubteth is damned if he eat, because he eateth not of faith: for whatsoever is not of faith is sin." This book is putting forth the love of the Living Truth, of whom is the Lord our God who was sent from His Majesty the Almighty God and Father of all creation. To not believe this mystery which is written in this book is to be deliberately containing the untruthful spirit. (II Thessalonians.2:7,12.) "For the mystery of iniquity doth already work: only he who now letteth will let, until he be taken out of the way. And then shall that wicked be revealed, whom the Lord shall consume with the spirit of His mouth, and shall destroy with the brightness of His coming: Even him, whose coming is after the working of satan with all power and signs and lying wonders. And with all deceivableness of unrighteousness in them that perish; because they receive not the love of the Truth, that they might be saved. And for this cause God shall send them strong delusion, that they should believe a lie: That they all might be damned who believed not the Truth, but had pleasure in unrighteousness."

May the Grace of our God, the Lord Jesus Christ,
the sweet communion of the Holy Spirit be
upon you all, in the name of Jesus;
A-men: